MY GARDEN, THE CITY AND ME

MY GARDEN, THE CITY AND ME

Rooftop Adventures in the Wilds of London

HELEN BABBS

TIMBER PRESS
PORTLAND • LONDON

Published in 2011 by Timber Press, Inc.
The Haseltine Building
133 S.W. Second Avenue, Suite 450
Portland, Oregon 97204-3527
www.timberpress.com

2 The Quadrant
135 Salusbury Road
London NW6 6RJ
www.timberpress.co.uk

ISBN-13: 978-1-60469-167-2

Printed in the United States of America

Catalogue records for this book are available from the British Library
and the Library of Congress.

Contents

PREFACE

What sorts of Londoners grow vegetables? Ones that live in domestic bliss, whatever that may be? Ones that are married, have a dog and can conjure up home-grown culinary masterpieces without a bead of sweat or an angry word? Well, that's definitely not me. I don't live in circumstances I'd describe as even faintly blissful. My kitchen is pokey and my bathroom borders on mouldy. I rent my room; I don't have a husband, a cute canine or a proper garden. If I'm honest, I'm not even a very good cook.

I am, however, guilty of being a sometime melancholic and an over-thinker. Someone who courts doubts that drum out of tune. But I think we probably all have at least one thing that we can get sickeningly pleased about. Something that's consistently cheering.

Green space, wildlife and the anatomy of London, my home city, are definitely three things I find heartening. When all is gloomy, there are camouflaged places to escape to – ones with thick foliage and rolling London views. And then there is my rooftop.

This is a book about the glory of growing things, about nature and the ecology of a city. It's about a side of London that's not often explored, and it's also somewhat about being here in your unsettled mid-twenties. Its intention is to reveal how much wildlife a city can support, and hopefully inspire you to see built-up spaces in new ways. It's also an ode to how satisfying gardening can be, no matter how hopeless at it you are. It's by no means a how-to guide, more the story of a first gardening year and the adventures that ensued.

So, welcome to my imperfect world, where – in a landscape that's unrelentingly urban – plants grow, creatures roam and I attempt to seek out idylls in the chaos.

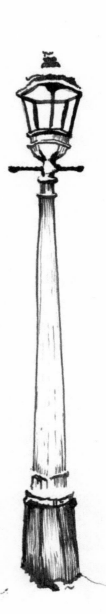

WINTER

1. Early January

My bedroom has two doors in it. One is the usual sort – an internal entrance and exit, the way to the kitchen, the bathroom, the street – but the other one opens out onto my downstairs neighbours' kitchen roof. This one leads to an escape, a hanging Mary Poppins-style place, all chimney stacks, tree tops and huge skies. Other people's gardens lie below the roof, while the backs of houses surround it. From here you can see no roads and no cars, but you can see a sycamore tree and, behind it, a random patch of wilderness, a marooned island of knotty tree and bush that's strangely managed to escape being built on.

I've lived here for a while now, renting a room in what has got to be one of the smallest apartments in the world. My flatmate and I share a tiny, postage stamp sized place but, despite the spatial limitations, we like it here. We moved out of the house from hell to this little slice of calm at the end of a charmed cul-de-sac just over a year ago. We've exchanged damp problems, mice infestations and high maintenance flatmates for something that's a lot less hard work. The flat is in a particularly chaotic bit of north London, sandwiched between the Camden and Holloway Roads, but somehow, when you turn the corner into our street, the city is less loud and there's peace.

Although you can hear traffic, aeroplanes and sirens from the roof, the dominant sounds are often the wind, birds and domestic life. This is a space watched over by many private windows, of people indulging in washing up daydreams and contemplative cigarettes. The roof garden isn't remote or silent, but this actually makes it more interesting. I like to think of it balancing on a cloud of city noise and dust, part of something bigger but also a little bit removed.

When I say roof garden perhaps I'm exaggerating somewhat, as it's quite sparse. I began experimenting with growing things last year but wasn't terribly successful. This year things are going to be different. I'm going to transform what is currently an unimpressive, small outdoor space into an organic, aerial, edible garden full of fruit, vegetables and flowers – a true living room.

The rooftop is like a large balcony, just under three metres square in size. The sycamore tree is my nearest neighbour and it's frequented by several squirrels and many birds. The roof gets sun all day long and the sunsets are particularly brilliant at this time of year, when the leaves are gone and tree skeletons are silhouetted against glowing winter skies.

It's currently home to a table and chairs, a couple of lavender plants and three small heathers. It's a bit empty and rather bleak, but I'm looking at it as a blank canvas where great things will happen.

As is traditional in winter, I'm dedicating my first few months as a wildlife friendly, organic kitchen gardener to planning. I'm reading books, writing lists, drawing strange diagrams and considering what essential hardware to buy, like secateurs, a trowel, perhaps even a broom. I really am starting from scratch – last year's token planting was done with a child's blue plastic spade I bought at the seaside, which is more suited to sandcastle construction than horticulture. So far the main priorities for the garden project are that it's cheap, doesn't swallow too much time, and produces fairly instant results. Patience isn't one of my strongest virtues and I want to see the roof developing into something special quickly.

I moved to London when I was eighteen to go to university. Now in my mid-twenties, I'm a committed city girl with no gardening experience but I do feel a strong connection to the natural world. I'm fascinated by urban wildlife and am keen to do something environmentally positive in an age of eco doom and gloom. I want to invest something into the place where I live, to do something creative and weave living walls around the building that I currently call home. The idea that my fingers will turn green seems quite fantastical in a way, but I love the thought of turning a little bit of city grey into a little bit of city green.

One fifth of London is garden. There are over three million of them and they'd span an area equivalent to the size of 268 Hyde Parks if you stuck them all together in one great lump. That's a massive amount of space with enormous potential. We all know that plants soak up carbon dioxide, tree planting being the most popular way for us to ease our environmental consciences after taking a flight. But green spaces are more than just CO_2 sponges. They provide valuable shelter and shade, as well as soaking up excess water.

In urban areas, with their canyons of concrete and cliff faces of brick and mortar, the effects of global warming are more keenly felt. Hard surfaces absorb heat, meaning built-up areas get hotter faster and then take an age to cool down. The urban heat island effect is a killer. Hard surfaces also don't absorb water, so the risk of flooding is increased. Sudden downpours result in great lakes on city streets with nowhere to go. Any urban space that's green and absorbent is therefore useful when the weather is hot or wet.

It's easy to feel fairly despondent when thinking about challenges like climate change, but filling our world capital cities with wild and beautiful gardens is a great way to do something constructive. The typical London garden is modest in size, and many people who rent or live in high-rise buildings don't have a garden to call their own. But Londoners are starting to grow things wherever they can. Shared community plots are hugely popular and waiting lists for allotments are years long. Living roofs and vegetated walls can be spotted on some sky-scraping buildings, while numerous rooftops, balconies and window ledges are hosting everything from a few herbs to chicken coops, beehives and mature trees.

Recent research into the number and anatomy of London's gardens has revealed how valuable they are but has also highlighted the scale of garden loss. Front gardens have been paved into driveways, while back gardens have become the victims of extensions or are dominated by patio slabs and decking. London is often heralded as one of the greenest cities in the world, universally celebrated for its vast swathes of parkland and its bijou leafy squares, but neglecting the value of the city's private gardens is a crime. Garden loss, in an era of climatic change and declining biodiversity, is an urban tragedy. Wildlife needs the habitats that gardens provide, while city people need the health-giving peacefulness of easily accessible outdoor spaces.

Creating productive as well as wildlife friendly green spaces also makes perfect sense. Food growing has numerous benefits, from saving money to making seasonal, healthy eating easier. Home-grown crops, cultivated organically and sustainably, provide pollen and nectar for insects and sustenance for humans, while cutting out chemicals and endless food miles. As I ate my breakfast this morning, I heard politicians on the radio suggesting that food security is as big an issue as energy security for the western world.

In the context of climate change, garden loss and decreasing food security, it seems my roof has no excuse but to make an effort to become a card-carrying garden. It's a mere dot on the London map, all three metres square of it, but if we all turn a dot into a garden the joined-up results will be far from inconsequential.

2. Early February

I've been thinking about the kinds of plants I'd like on the roof, focusing my thoughts on things that will make the garden a slice of paradise for wildlife as well as me. Unsurprisingly, I'm finding myself attracted to fruit and vegetables that are notoriously easy to grow. It looks like the runner bean will work for me on several levels. It's fast growing, low maintenance and will quickly coat a large section of wall in magic bean stalks. The flowers are a real favourite of bees and butterflies, while the vegetables themselves will crop for weeks and provide me with many meals. Runner beans also fare well in pots, which is essential as every plant I grow will have to cope with an entirely container-bound life. Overall, my reading has revealed that anyone can grow beans.

It's early February, it's freezing cold and it's the weekend. With all my thoughts firmly bean shaped, I've left London in pursuit of seeds, sporting my woolliest hat and clutching a short wish list. I'm going to an event called Seedy Sunday in Hove on the south coast. It's a large, annual community seed swap and sounds like the perfect place to go seed shopping. After the initial heat of ambitious New Year's resolutions, my aim of growing a set of green fingers has been feeling fairly abstract. There's been lots of thinking but absolutely no doing, so taking a day trip to the seaside to buy seeds from the hands of the people that grew them seems like a good idea.

It was Seedy Sunday's playful name that first caught my attention but, after finding out more, I was hooked by the idea of people coming together to swap seeds, in a bid to promote community growing and to protect plant biodiversity. The event and subsequent campaign was started years ago by the Brighton and Hove organic gardening group, after members stumbled upon a seed swap in Canada.

The minute they got back to the UK, the organizers started planning their first swap here. The annual event has grown and grown, best illustrated by the fact it's moved from a small community hall in Brighton to the imposing Hove Town Hall. The concept has been embraced by people across the country and smaller scale Seedy Sundays now happen all over the place.

Activists warn that thousands of unlisted garden varieties are disappearing and with them goes some of the genetic raw material that will allow plants to adapt and survive in the future. The campaign is all about protesting against a predominance of large-scale growing and retailing, and rests on the belief that, by growing open pollinated or heritage plants and then saving and swapping the seeds, growers can keep local seed varieties alive and boost biodiversity.

The air is ice cold and the wind fierce, but the light is lovely – a fuzzy, pale pink haze is hanging over a dark grey winter sea. Hove is full of colourful bobble hats and cheeks bitten rosy by wind that's laced with snow. Lots of people are out, taking the Sunday sea air and walking the beach hut-lined stretch towards Brighton. But I'm not here to indulge myself with coastal strolls, I'm here to do some serious seed shopping.

The hall is full of people and is really noisy. I confess, as a frostbitten novice grower, out of her London bubble and attending her first seed swap solo, it's all slightly overwhelming. Seeing so much expertise and enthusiasm for gardening in one place, and just so many seeds and possibilities, makes me realize how little I know about anything when it comes to growing things. I have my list with me though, which is helping to keep me calm. At the top are runner bean seeds (but which variety?) and also on there are radishes, herbs and salads. But, if I'm honest, my rooftop plan is suddenly feeling rather undeveloped and maybe even a little vague.

What is most appealing about the swap are the quirky seed names and homemade packaging, both of which are going to influence my purchases. Names like 'Drunken Woman' and 'Fat Lazy Blonde' lettuce, 'Flamingo Beet' chard, 'Hungry Gap' cabbage, 'Hungarian Hot Wax' peppers and 'Nun's Belly Button' bean seeds are all making me smile. The early 'Red Rum' runner beans I've fixed upon are wrapped up in thick polka dot paper, with inky instructions written in a flourish on the front by a sweeping hand. And so it begins, with my first seed choices for the roof being dictated by the romance of the words and the prettiness of the packets rather than by anything more sensible.

SKELETONS IN THE SNOW

It's late and the roof is looking particularly stunning at the moment. The snow's been coming down solidly for hours, travel chaos has ensued and Londoners are collectively shivering, but the city is looking lovely under a thick frozen blanket. It's nighttime and the light polluted sky is making the snow glow yellow. Peering out at the roof through a crack in my curtains well after it should be dark, the garden is infused with a soupy twilight.

Such deep freezes don't lead to much gardening activity, not in my bit of north London anyway. I may have taken in a little seaside seed shopping at the weekend, but it's still far too early to be subjecting myself or any new plantlets to long periods out on the ice slicked roof. Everything out there looks fantastic though, altered by snow and frost, not just in appearance but also in smell and sound. However, it's actually a brilliant time of year to spot wildlife. While many species do hibernate over winter, there are still lots of wildlife watching opportunities. With trees bare of their leaves, the chances of seeing the silhouette of an owl cutting across a moonlit sky are greatly increased. Watching birds feeding in the dim half-light of an early winter morning is a joy, and spying a fox foraging, as frost thickens and glisters in the evening gloom, has a special, chilly charm.

One of the most eye-catching and out of the ordinary sights at this time of year is the flash of a red admiral. These butterflies normally spend winter in sheltered places like the dark corners of outbuildings, but on warm days they can become active again and be seen fluttering about. Unusual weather is affecting many species' hibernation patterns, with unexpectedly high temperatures sometimes tempting them to venture out in the depths of winter. Hard to imagine on such a snowy night as this, but it is becoming more common.

Butterflies are delicate creatures and are vulnerable if they emerge at this time of year because they burn up vital fat stores searching for nectar. One way to cater for these early risers is to plant winter bloomers like heathers, winter flowering jasmine or honeysuckle. In an emergency, a dish of sugar water left out for an active butterfly may help keep its energy levels up. It's not just butterflies that are increasingly seen at this time of year, some bumblebee nests in southern parts of the UK are now active throughout winter too. Worker bees might be seen gathering pollen from flowers and, on warmer days, the larger queen bee could possibly be found hunting for potential nesting sites.

It turns out that the plants I already have on the roof are doing much to aid wildlife at what is a difficult time in terms of food and cover. The heather is a source of nectar for any insects that brave the cold, while my lavender bush is not only providing a little bit of much needed winter texture and colour, it's also providing valuable shelter to those that need it.

This is of course the time of year when birds rely on humans for extra sustenance. I've started leaving out bruisey apples, nuts, seeds and fat. As the snow continues to fall, I'm thinking about stringing chains of monkey nuts around the roof, studding apples with sunflower seeds and fashioning a bird feeder out of an old plastic bottle. Maybe I'll even bake a bird cake and set it in half a coconut. I've noticed that small flocks of house sparrows are hanging around by the roof at the moment; they're generally active in the middle of the day when the weak sun is at its strongest. They're really noisy and seem to love the sycamore and one particular bush in a neighbour's garden best.

The house sparrow, affectionately known as the Cockney sparrow round these parts, used to be a common sight in London but it's become far rarer of late. Funnily enough, the largest group of them is now to be found at London Zoo, where the little brown birds favour hanging out with their more exotic cousins in the tropical bird house. They are often seen in the gorilla kingdom, too.

Grand views of, and especially from, green spaces are one of the best things about London and perhaps even more so in winter. This is a city where one can lose long minutes standing and staring out over undulating urban sprawl, admiring vistas made up of buildings and monuments ancient and modern, all peppered with trees and grass. In winter, the views change – the sky is emptier and seems vaster, the sun is low and there is more glare and sparkle.

As a north Londoner, the classic views for me have to be from Primrose Hill and Kenwood and Parliament Hills on Hampstead Heath. Walking in these two, very different, green spaces – one a wild expanse, one small and clipped – I find they're quieter and prettier in their thin winter clothes.

Tree skeletons are easily my favourite thing about winter. There's a tree on the Heath that sits on top of a gentle hill and sometimes casts a spectacular and complicated shadow against a sky that is so bright it makes eyes ache and the scene pixelate. It's easier to identify trees in the bare months – oaks look like big, old brains while lime trees are gloriously droopy. I most love the London plane trees, still decked with their furry baubles long after twelfth night has passed and the Christmas decorations have been taken down.

The plane is the most common tree in the city. Growing wide and tall, it can be found in all manner of parks and squares, as well as lining streets from the centre to the suburbs. The plane's

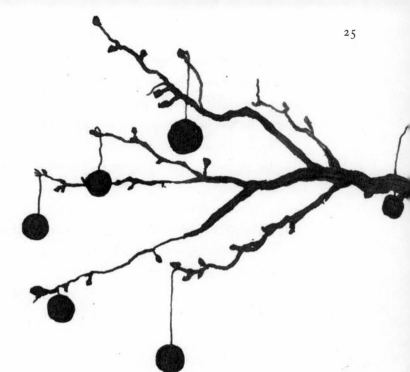

peeling, flaky bark is key to its success in London. By shedding its skin, the tree protects itself from pollution. Its glossy leaves also help – grime is easily washed off their shiny surfaces by rain, which London gets lots of. The furry nuts that cover the tree look especially striking in winter, when spiky clusters sway decoratively from bare branches.

The London plane is actually a non-native hybrid, but the species has been growing in the UK for hundreds of years. The first record of the tree dates from 1670. Many of London's were planted over two hundred years ago, and are still going strong despite the sooty and cramped conditions they've had to contend with. The city's oldest plane trees can be found in Berkeley Square in Mayfair – they were planted way back in 1789, while the largest tree can be found on the banks of the Thames at Richmond.

In his compelling biography of London, Peter Ackroyd says the plane is the single most important reason why London has been apostrophized as a 'city of trees' with 'solemn shapes' and 'glooms Romantic'.

3. Mid March

There have been moments of late when it's felt like spring may soon be here. Dragging myself out of bed at an unearthly hour earlier this week, I took a night bus over to the East Reservoir in Hackney to watch day break over the water. At a quarter past six all was muted, the cold air full of wisps of mist, the still pool a pinky grey. By half past, the sky began to gently yellow and warm to orange.

The sun started to peek over the reed bed, turning the dusty-looking plants copper and black. It rose as a burning red disc with a lighter halo of cloud sitting above, angled like a jauntily placed cap with a trail of light spilling away from it. Dark silhouettes of resting water birds bobbed on the lava-like water. The sky burned with fire and yet it was still deeply cold. Frost sparkled in the flames of dawn. Later that morning, I sat and watched great crested grebes – water birds that couple by performing a hypnotic pair-bonding dance. Soon they will nest and then they will swim the reservoir carrying striped chicks on their backs.

A few days later, I stayed up all night watching an epic piece of theatre. After the final curtain and some breakfast, I stumbled home in a dreamlike fog as the sun was rising. Walking north as the sky brightened, I felt that winter was slowly coming to an end. There was a new warmth in the air that morning that hinted at spring.

As the new season suggests itself, it's perhaps time to make a few more decisions about the roof. Returning to those strange diagrams I'd been creating earlier in the year, I've been developing more of a plan of the shape I'd like the garden to take, deciding on the sorts of things I want to plant and thinking about how I might grow them.

Something I've been considering is the type of compost I'm going to use. The roof is just that, a rooftop, with no connection at all to the earth. It's a flat, artificial surface, designed to keep the elements out, not to nurture plants. Everything will be in pots and I will have to buy all the compost I use, as I don't have any space on the roof to make my own.

My local council collects food and garden waste, which means I can recycle those things, but then I can't reap the rewards in terms of a free and ready supply of rich soil. Buying compost is going to be expensive and also something of a logistical nightmare. The stuff weighs a tonne. There's also more than one product on offer and I need to make good decisions – my compost choice has to reflect my desires to be organic and kind to the natural world.

Peat, still the primary ingredient in much multi-purpose compost, is the issue here and I've been doing my research. Researching bogs, doesn't exactly sound glamorous, does it? But when I've told people about it, they've lit up. Perhaps I've been confessing to somewhat special individuals but I'm not sure that's it, because peatlands truly are extraordinary places. The more I discover about the wild exoticism of the bog, the more it seems clear that I should be shunning peat products.

One friend, someone I definitely regard as an urbanite, went all misty-eyed over the 'b' word, reminiscing about a few months he'd spent in the Hebrides, off the west Scottish coast, doing wildlife surveying. He described the rich, peaty landscape as a true wilderness and as isolated as you can get in the British Isles. Another person I told got overexcited about the idea of bog people, the ancient bodies that were pulled out of peatlands after being preserved by the uniquely acidic, oxygen-less earth.

Unfortunately, bogs have been consistently destroyed and degraded for decades. People have used peat for centuries, and while hand cutting it for fuel can be sustainable as the peat is often able to gradually re-form, the industrial-scale stripping of peat for horticultural products is a real problem.

It started in the fifties with the rise of the garden centre, an explosion in amateur gardening and an increasing trend to grow things in containers. It would be silly to suggest that peat isn't an effective growing medium. It's good at holding air and water and is sterile, easy to store and relatively cheap. Since the seventies, it's been the compost of choice for nearly all growers and this has had terrible environmental consequences for boggy lands that store large amounts of carbon dioxide and form vital wildlife habitats.

The living creatures that call peat home are fascinating and the plant, moss and lichen life is nothing short of exotic. There are the carnivorous and brightly coloured sundew and butterwort plants, which have something almost tropical about them; there's the delicate beauty of minty-smelling bog myrtle, rare bog rosemary and bog asphodel, not to mention the multicoloured and multi-textured patchwork of sphagnum mosses. Bogs support various birdlife as well as dragonflies, damselflies, frogs and lizards. The sight of the magnificently hairy caterpillar of the dark tussock moth is something to behold.

As well as being peat-free, the roof is also going to be organic. The devastation unleashed on the natural world with the introduction of pesticides is a horror story and I couldn't justify using chemicals in my garden. One of the privileges of growing your own food is the power it gives you to decide not to wreak havoc on ecosystems through your actions.

Choosing to have an organic roof isn't a tough decision but it does have implications. The fact that the plants are going to be in pots means they're going to need extra nourishment. I'll need to choose compost that is not only peat-free but also injected with some organic magic ingredients that will make my crops a success. Such compost is available but it tends to be more expensive.

Another implication is that any pest control methods employed are going to have to adhere to the organic rules. No sprays, no slug pellets and no other miracle cures. To be honest, I can see myself being quite slack on the pest control front – I can't imagine getting that worked up about sharing my plants with a few insects, but let's see how I feel when something I've grown from seed becomes the victim of an aphid attack.

As well as being peat-free and organic, I'd like to ensure the roof is also a great place to sit and to entertain. I want to be able to lie back and feel like I'm surrounded by greenery. The roof is small but I'd like to keep enough space free to be able to invite one or two people round for drinks. I'd like to plant in hanging baskets, grow bags and ordinary plant pots. I'd like to grow things that climb and things that creep. I'd like the roof to be busy with bees and butterflies. Crop-wise, I'd like lots of salad leaves and herbs but also an abundance of red fruits and a 'Red Rum' runner bean mountain.

CREATURES

The roof is already a stop-off point for some local wildlife. I guess it's a good vantage point from which to spy on other beasts and generally check out the lay of the land. I have a pair of blackbirds that visit regularly and often, plus a squirrel that likes lounging on my fence posts and rooting through any pots. The occasional wood pigeon makes an appearance too, dropping down now and then from a favoured perch in the sycamore tree. Far prettier and plumper than the more common feral pigeon, these birds are surprisingly large and always cause a stir when they stop by.

The range of wild creatures that inhabit London is something that excites and interests me a lot. The fact that they are surviving, adapting and even thriving in the most built-up of places is utterly brilliant. Over the last few weeks a seal has been seen sprawling in St Saviour's Dock, a small Thames wharf that's literally minutes from Tower Bridge. Most days, she hauls herself out onto a sunny platform in the river, which used to be the sole property of a now disgruntled swan.

Wide-eyed and gregarious, the common seal is the most widespread of all pinnipeds (fin-footed mammals). They are found across the north Atlantic and Pacific Oceans, but aren't terribly common in England's capital city. It's not unknown to see the odd, lone seal bobbing in the Thames during the winter, but each time one is spotted it still causes ripples of excitement and can often make the evening news, especially if a photographer catches one looking particularly cute.

Preferring rocky outcrops, mudflats, gravelly beaches and even coastal piers, seals may be driven upriver by bad weather and the promise of a decent lunch. They like to bask, hauling themselves out of the water to lounge around for hours on end, typically in small groups, but also alone and in mass gangs. A good haul-out site will be sheltered from land predators and extreme weather, as well as being close to deep water and therefore a good supply of food. During the moulting season, they can haul out for epic twelve-hour stretches. They often adopt a head-up, tail-up pose.

They're opportunistic when it comes to food, hunting fish, molluscs and crustaceans, all of which can be found in the now clean Thames. Only fifty years ago, the river was so polluted that it couldn't sustain a single fish, while these days it supports around 125 different types.

As March progresses and the weather improves, I've been finding all manner of elaborate excuses to spend as much time as possible in the park. Regent's Park and Kensington Gardens, both just minutes in different directions from the madness of Oxford Street, have had an extraordinary magnetism for me of late. Warmer than most places due to their central London locations, they're already becoming carpeted with early spring flowers, which is endlessly cheering, but their main allure lies in the fact that they're both hosting some feathered wildlife of note at the moment.

On an island in the boating lake at Regent's Park is London's most central heronry, with a selection of trees holding huge nests where the pterodactyl-like birds are sitting on eggs. An old lady, a nun in fact, regularly visits the lake bearing sprats for the herons' lunch. Normally solitary eaters, the herons know her well; they flock to the tiny woman and it's quite a sight to see her lost in a tangle of long limbs and sharp beaks. I've taken to walking by the lake in the late morning and sitting on a bench nearby to watch feeding time.

Although not a rare bird, the grey heron looks exotic. Its gaunt, sharp shape, dagger-like beak, stone-still patience and deliberate, stalking movements all make it seem like a beast from another time. It can be seen all year round, most often statue-still on the water's edge, silently waiting for something delicious to spear with its beak. It will stand motionless on one or two legs, with its neck hunched into its body or extended to full length.

The birds start breeding from February, with fancy neck movements and much beak snapping. Heron nests are large, platform constructions and are easy to spot in tall trees that are still bare of leaves. The spectacular heronries at Walthamstow Reservoirs in north east London are the largest in the capital.

On a clear morning, when the sun isn't long up, they're a brilliant place to be. The water reflects back a scene that is both odd and beautiful. Crowds of wild birds are silhouetted in naked trees, ringed by roads, train lines and the shapes of the city.

Back in the centre of town and in chichi Kensington Gardens, on the borders of Hyde Park, a tawny owl couple have just had four owlets. The birds are easy to spot in the old oak and plane trees, sleeping out during the day and hunting by night. The baby birds are chubby balls of grey fluff, with dark eyes, tiny beaks and long talons. Although still young and vulnerable, they're already good climbers and can fly from tree to tree.

Those that stumble upon these secret-ish spectacles walk away from them faintly dazzled. Who would have thought central London could boast flocks of herons feeding together in a chaotic squabble or a pair of tawny owls nurturing a new family, with all handsome members clearly visible during the day? Tawny owls are always one of the first birds to have chicks each year, often having them as early as February but sometimes later if the weather is harsh, like it has been this year. The owlets are impossibly sweet and their presence in the park is a clear sign that spring has almost sprung.

THE COMMUTE

On my daily commute from north to south London the human wildlife can be fascinating, but there's more to the packed morning landscape than just people and the manmade. I wait for the bus with a flock of busy gulls and pigeons, fed daily by a lady who brings them a substantial, if a little stale breakfast, carefully wrapped in a plastic bag. The growing bus stop crowd watches the birds swarm and settle around her with shrieks of thanks.

London was once a city of rivers, but most are now lost or have disappeared deep underground. Every day I form part of the cargo of a tall red ship that sails the course of what was the River Fleet, downhill to the Thames. Sometimes and somehow, if you let your mind wander

enough, it's still possible to feel the flow of this lost waterway, for so long now encased in brick and piping, coursing beneath the city's thick concrete crust.

As our bus journeys southwards through King's Cross, the passenger whose eyes are not glued to a morning free-sheet can spot bursts of growth amongst the rusty gas towers, pockets of insistent wilderness forcing themselves up between rail tracks, and then the sudden flash of the canal, glinting blade-like in pale early sun.

We head down Farringdon Road, following the lost tributary's path, past Smithfield market, the meat mecca that polluted the old river to extinction. The grey is persistent on this stretch, with concessionary street trees imprisoned in cast-iron cages within snatches of gravelly soil. But wildness approaches as the Fleet speeds us closer to its final destination.

The moment we meet the Thames at Blackfriars, something changes, as if everyone onboard lets out a deep breath as we travel onto the bridge. Suddenly London opens out in front us. We can see in all directions – a wide screen panorama of space in super high definition. The light changes, there is depth and shade, shifting shadows chase clouds across the water's surface. The sky extends its arms with a long, lazy stretch. It's not a commute, it's like reaching the top of a mountain. I want to throw open the double-decker bus windows, drink in the brackish air and taste the sea.

SPRING

4. Late March into April

I'm dedicating the first tentative days of spring to surveying the rooftop and making some final decisions so I can get on with the business of growing stuff. I've been spending some time simply watching the roof and thinking back to how climatic conditions were up here last year, in an attempt to understand the space a bit better before I start gardening in earnest.

Unless there's a raging storm or temperatures have dropped bone-chillingly low, the roof is usually a mild place. As the weather slowly gets more cheerful, it'll become an ideal growing environment. It's south-facing and gets soaked in sun all day long. It's also kept warm by the external wall of my flat and the heat that rises from the kitchen in the flat below.

Exposure to wind can be a problem for aerial gardens, but mine's not that high up and it's sheltered from strong blasts by the surrounding houses and trees. A metre-high slatted wooden fence runs around it, providing something of a windbreak. The only real limitation I have is lack of space and the fact that I'm gardening on a flat roof, so excessively heavy weight could turn out to be a problem.

A design for the garden is starting to emerge. Nothing rigid – no doubt it will change and adapt to circumstance; I just need something of a plan to get myself started. I'd like the area immediately to the right of my bedroom door to have tomatoes and cucumbers, while in the far right corner and along the back fence there could be various herbs and greens. The far left corner will be dedicated to sweet-scented flowers, with a focus on ones that attract insects. I also like the idea of having a nut tree.

My small round table and its three chairs will remain along the left-hand edge of the roof, nestling nicely next to the fragrant area, with a hanging basket of strawberries swinging above. I'd like sweet peas to climb up the fence beside the table too. The near left corner, underneath the bathroom window, will be a potting and storage area. Finally, the space running along the wall of my flat – the external wall of the bathroom and my bedroom – will be where I grow the runner beans. They can clamber up all over it and turn it green.

So starting tomorrow, I'm planning to plant my beans, plus a mixture of cherry, classic and plum tomatoes and various mixed salad leaves, including rocket and 'Drunken Woman' lettuce. I want one container to have a hot pink theme, so it will be planted with 'French Breakfast' radishes and 'Flamingo Beet' chard seeds.

The table is there so I can entertain my friends as well as myself – I want to grow strawberries, mint and cucumber so I have all the ingredients on hand for Pimm's and lemonade. I'm attempting to grow the cucumber from seed but will get the strawberries and mint as small plants. Herbs are definitely essential and hopefully easy. I'm going to try sweet Genovese basil, coriander, flat-leaved parsley and purple chives from seed, and I'll also buy rosemary as a plant and a small bay tree. I'm hoping to get cuttings of lemon balm and oregano.

So, full of grand ambitions for tomorrow, I'm off to the garden centre today. I've roped in a friend with a car because there's no way I'll be able to lug the amount of compost I want to buy back home on the bus. I have all the seeds I need now, bought at the seed swap in Hove, and also freebies collected from gardening magazines and donated by friends and family. As well as plants and compost, I want to buy a few window box style planters, three large pots, a grow bag and a hanging basket. I've acquired a few odd pots already and I'm going to start all the seedlings off in small containers I've collected over the last few months – things like yoghurt pots, milk bottles, fruit punnets and food trays.

SOILY AT LAST

Post my garden centre trip, I've been getting properly soily at last. I've been sowing seeds with abandon and my bedroom is now more plant nursery than sleeping quarters. I've constructed a rather wobbly shelving unit to keep my future seedlings on indoors, and the seeds I've planted directly outside are being protected from cold spells and inquisitive squirrels by old clear plastic containers.

Although the danger of a late frost remains, it's been gorgeous on the roof recently. I took a luxurious couple of days off work last week and there was early spring sunshine, hastily planted daffodils nodding in a gentle breeze, glimpses of my downstairs' neighbours' snowdrops and endless cups of fresh coffee – perfection.

I'd forgotten quite how much I love having this space to escape to and lose hours in. It's not so appealing in winter, when I find myself peering out of my bedroom window at it rather than actually spending much time out there. But suddenly it's charming again and I've been out on the roof as much as I can. I'm really glad I planted a few spring bulbs during an inspired moment in the colder months, as the daffodils that are now dotted about the place look really cheerful.

I have a few new plants – the strawberries and all the herbs I had planned, plus more lavender, a bushy jasmine, a climbing

honeysuckle and a lupin with star-shaped leaves that have been sparkling with balls of dew every morning. These plants tick all the right boxes – they're attractive, they smell great and bees love them.

Bee populations have suffered serious declines recently, so it's a priority to provide these important pollinators with a food source. They're not just providers of honey for our toast: they're crucial to agriculture and worth millions to the global economy. Without bees, there would be few flowering crops and our food plants depend upon them. Every kitchen gardener and allotment holder needs bees in order to be productive.

Fossils show that bees have been around for 150 million years and there's evidence that humans have been beekeeping for at least 6,000. Bees are amazing – these tiny creatures that never sleep can achieve speeds of up to 20mph and a worker bee will fly 500 miles in its short lifetime.

Only four types of London bees actually make honey, but all species have a vital role to play in terms of pollination. Some species form small colonies of a few hundred individuals, while honey bees form huge ones of as many as 20,000, with each bee the offspring of a single queen. She lays all the eggs, while worker bees collect the pollen and nectar that keep the colony supplied with food.

I visited an aerial beekeeper who keeps two hives on her roof terrace in Bermondsey last week. I think she and her husband might be fading eighties pop stars that I failed to recognize.

They were wealthy, eccentric and gave the impression of having partied hard in their youth. These days, they're passionate about bees.

Each of their hives can hold thousands of honey bees, which fly south on warm mornings, in pursuit of nourishment. They return weighed down with pollen and nectar, the last often sourced from London's many lime trees. The beekeeper delightedly described how the bees communicate where the best ambrosia is to be found via their 'waggle dance', which somehow maps out a route that a watching bee can follow. A wet summer last year resulted in a low honey yield, then the beekeeper's entire colony was wiped out by the bitterly cold winter that followed. Sad but absolutely not giving up, she's now on the hunt for some replacement bees and will soon be making honey again.

As well as honey bees, there are also over two hundred species of solitary bees and wasps, which lay their eggs in cells hidden away in soft sand, soil or mortar, providing each egg with its own food supply. Perhaps the best-known solitary bee is the leaf-cutter, which cuts neat little semi-circles from the leaves and flowers of roses. They're distinctive because of the bright orange pollen brush on their back legs. London is also home to the spring flower, mason and lawn solitary bees. Bumblebees are larger, fuzzier and more docile creatures that live in small colonies. London has several different species of these as well, including common carder, red-tailed, buff-tailed, white-tailed, early nesting and garden bumblebees.

As a general rule, bees love daisy- and bell-shaped single flowers – double flowers don't provide nectar for insects. The flowers on many fruit and vegetable crops are firm favourites of bees – beans, peas and fragrant herbs are loved, as are apples, currants and raspberries. If there's space in or around a vegetable plot, flowers like azaleas, bluebells, forget-me-nots, foxgloves, lupins and primroses will also help to attract bees.

Companion planting, a traditional method of growing different plants together for mutual benefits, like extra nutrients or protection from harsh weather and pests, can make vegetable gardens mutually good for bees and produce alike. For example, nasturtiums grown among brassicas will protect the latter from caterpillars – caterpillars will choose to eat nasturtium leaves rather than cabbages, while the nasturtiums' vibrant, velveteen flowers will attract bees. Chives or sage amongst a crop of carrots will ward off aphids and are also great for bees, which are then on hand to pollinate other crops.

A HAZEL CALLED HUGH

Today I'm going to buy myself that little nut tree I've been dreaming of. I'm heading east to Columbia Road market in Hoxton, where discerning Londoners go to buy fresh cut flowers, bargain plants and hearty breakfasts. It's a twenty-minute bus ride from my house and you know you're getting close when you start spotting people walking the streets with their arms full of plants, or cars driving past with foliage spilling out of their windows.

A narrow street that cuts from manic Old Street to the middle of Hackney Road, Columbia Road is lined with quirky shops and eateries. On Sundays the road is virtually impassable as it's taken over by the flower market – an assault of noise, colour and leafy smells. People swarm to this place, where Cockney flower sellers hawk their vegetal wares.

I've looked at hazel trees in garden centres but balked at the price tags. I simply refuse to pay £30 or more. I arrive at Columbia Road, immerse myself in the crush and emerge at the end of it the triumphant owner of a tiny hazel that stands about a metre tall and has curly branches and lots of buds. He cost me a fiver and I'm calling him Hugh. Sitting awkwardly with him skimming the roof of the top deck of a bus, we attract a few smiles as we journey back to a roof and a bedroom that are both full of tiny sprouts. Yes, I have seedlings now, and I also have Hugh. Things are finally taking shape.

5. Mid April into May

Each morning and evening there's an inspection to see how much the seedlings have grown. Sometimes the inspections are mere minutes apart, when I'm feeling particularly keen or perhaps slightly overwrought. Work, family and boy troubles are all easily forgot when measuring a million miniature plants with a ruler.

My runner beans have just had a lucky escape from a snail attack. I'm currently teaching them about the world outside my flat, hardening them off and sending them on day trips to the roof. It's been drizzling all day and by nightfall the beans were looking luscious, their big floppy green leaves covered in damp. The snail just couldn't hold itself back. But I spotted it in time. I swear I heard it scream in frustration as I plucked it off. They're in for the night now, safe and sound. I am incredibly protective of all my plants after being in such close contact with them for the last six weeks, but it really is time I claimed my bedroom back – it's turning into a bit of a jungle. The plan is to move them outside permanently in the next few days.

March's seed planting means there are now sprouts all over the place. I have a healthy crop of tomato seedlings that will need potting on soon. I've also got rocket, loads of chives, one nasturtium and a couple of tiny basil plants. The basil's been through a lot so I'm proud of these two particular plants. On one of those rushed mornings where everything that could go wrong did, I collided with my pot of basil and sent it flying, spraying soil and seedlings all across the carpet. It was a setback for the basil, and a cue for some loud cursing from me, but it's determined and so am I.

It's lovely out on the roof now – the evenings are longer and the days are warmer. I spent a good few hours just basking last weekend, as the roof was transformed into an all-day April sun trap. The seeds I planted directly outside are coming along nicely. The beans and tomatoes are a lot smaller than those planted indoors, but I think they're going to be tough in the long run.

As well as snails, I've been dealing with increased interest from the local grey squirrels – they seem unable to resist freshly dug soil and I've found that, if plants aren't protected, they easily become the victims of frenzied squirrel digging attacks. It's difficult losing hard-grown plants to such violence. Seeds I've planted neatly in one container are also sprouting up in completely different ones. Some purple tree spinach has appeared far away from where it was originally sown. The squirrels clearly have opinions on what should be planted where and will dig things up and move them if they don't agree with my planting decisions. I like squirrels but their interfering habits are starting to drive me slightly wild.

Anyway, the radishes are shooting up, as is the coriander. Parsley is starting to appear now and I have four little sunflowers. The strawberry plants in the hanging basket have at least doubled in size and have buds, and the mint is going mad. I've been trying to grow some cucumber to complete my Pimm's planting plan but there's sadly still nothing happening in the cucumber pot.

I've recently decided that I should have a night corner on the roof. I already have jasmine and honeysuckle plants, which are all sprouty at the moment and will soon be fragrant in the evenings. I'm also going to plant some evening primroses and tobacco plants. Moths are attracted by these plants' sugary scents and pale colours, using both to navigate. A committed moon bather, I want my garden to be full of fragrant flowers that glow after dark and are loved by night-flying insects.

KING PEST

My four little sunflowers have been beheaded; each one is a snail-trail-covered stump. In response, I've been reading about pests and thinking a bit more seriously about pest control. Despite being sure no pest could ever ruffle my feathers, I'm discovering that it's actually really hard to turn a blind eye when your garden comes under attack. Is it possible to find redeeming features in pest species that would make them easier to live with?

It's hard to love them, but there's much about slugs and snails that is fascinating, if a little horrifying. For example, a single slug has 27,000 teeth, can stretch to twenty times its normal length and can travel unharmed across the edge of a razor blade. The ordinary garden snail is able to seal the entrance to its shell with a parchment-like barrier, known as an epiphragm, and go into a state of suspended animation where it can survive for several months without water. Impressive, no?

Slugs and snails are gastropods, meaning that they move by contracting their muscular stomachs, gliding on a layer of lubricating mucus. Both are also hermaphrodites – they have male and female reproductive organs and can actually mate with themselves if necessary. Thirty species of slugs are found in Britain and the average garden contains over 20,000 of them. The leopard slug is probably our most magnificent, with its unusual-looking skin markings and its twisting mating dance. It also eats other slugs, which must make it the gardener's friend.

The Roman snail, Britain's biggest, can be found in far south London on rare tracts of chalk grassland. It's so uncommon and highly protected that you need a license to even touch it. Its shell can grow to 5cm across and it lives for up to ten years. More minuscule, the banded snail is a good-looking beast, with bold, dark stripes streaking a shell that only grows to about 5mm across. London also supports the rare Desmoulin's whorl snail, the German hairy snail and the two-lipped door snail.

However much you might hate them, slugs and snails do have an important role to play in gardens, keeping green spaces balanced and healthy. They are crucial composters, eating dead and decaying plant and animal matter and releasing nutrients back into the soil. They also help disperse seeds and spores. They provide food for species like frogs, toads, birds and hedgehogs, all of which could do with help from wildlife friendly gardeners.

I'm staying committed to the no chemical rule so my methods of dissuading slugs and snails are going to hinge around checking crops regularly and picking off any offenders. I especially need to be on my guard after hours and when it's wet, as these slippery characters tend to be most active on damp nights. Cloches fashioned out of empty bottles can make great shields, and I'm going to put gravel around some plants because gastropods don't relish chafing their bellies on gritty surfaces.

I've discovered that I should probably be on my guard against pigeons as well, though this will depend somewhat on the type of crops I choose to grow. The wood pigeon is our largest and most common pigeon and is rather partial to peas and cabbages.

If pigeons were to descend on a brassica crop, it could be completely destroyed.

The only way to keep vulnerable plants safe is with netting, but this is effective, meaning that the vegetable grower and the pigeon can live in harmony, as long as the vegetable grower knows what the bird likes and takes suitable precautions. It sounds to me like netting could also be a useful way of protecting my plants from squirrels and their destructive digging habits.

Bold and agile, the urban squirrel is not an elusive beast. Found everywhere, particularly places where you'd rather they weren't, this species has adapted well to modern city life. Reports of obese and anti-social squirrels are widespread.

If you're feeling generous, you could label grey squirrels as entertaining or even impressive. They are able to leap more than six metres and are safe when falling from a height of nine. They have great eyesight and a keen sense of smell. Anyone who has tried to outwit a squirrel in their garden will know how quickly they learn.

They use their tails to communicate, twitching them if they're suspicious, and they mark regular routes with scent. They also use their tails as blankets on cold nights, curling up underneath them in compact spherical nests – a squirrel fact that is definitely verging on cute.

As someone who tries to feed the birds but only ends up

making my local squirrels even fatter, I've decided that believing that they're entertaining, impressive and cute is the best way of coping with the havoc they wreak on my roof. That and swearing loudly at them through the bathroom window, which helps but brings only temporary relief.

INSOMNIA AND SONG

I have rare moments of terrible insomnia, when I don't sleep well at all and my head is full of fog and glue. Tired and frustrated, I lie in bed listening to the patchwork of sounds that blow in off the roof – night buses steaming up Camden Road, wailing sirens of what feels like a thousand police chases, helicopters that circle and annoy like oversized blue-bottle flies. Happily, at this time of year the traffic's got competition.

The dawn chorus is compelling and a relief. In a place that can be dominated by traffic noise, to be awake in the early hours with the roar of what sounds like a thousand song birds spilling through the curtains is brilliant. Thoughts bat around and around my head and it becomes completely impossible to stay in bed.

The dawn chorus in London tends to begin in March, reaching a crescendo in May and June. It's linked to the birds' breeding seasons. It's all about defending territory and making one's presence felt in an area, and it's generally male birds that are responsible for the tunes. Blackbirds, robins and wrens are particularly vocal early on. Some say they pick morning to sing because it's quieter then and songs have more impact. This makes sense in London at least – at 4am all you can hear is birds, but in the middle of the day they'd have an awful lot more competition.

The roof is great when you're feeling shaky and can't sleep but I'm not sure it's anything other than bad behaviour to be out here at silly o'clock on a Monday morning, with a full week of work looming, attempting to record night noises on an old mini disc player I've pilfered from a friend. I'm standing here, trying not to cough, with the mini disc player catching everything in its tiny microphone, thinking how fetching the sycamore tree looks cast in shadow and echoing with birdsong. My rooftop world doesn't belong to me in the springtime midnight hours, every space has been claimed by a little winged creature with an enormous pair of lungs.

THE ASCENT

I'm going up a skyscraper in the middle of the City of London with a bunch of birdwatchers. We meet in the morning, on ground level, outside a towering building that houses offices and an expensive restaurant. It's one of the tallest buildings in London. Glass revolving doors sweep smartly clad people in and out. We gather out front then enter via the back doors. We take a service lift up forty-one floors. My ears pop. We walk up a couple of flights of stone stairs. Then up some tightly twisting metal steps. Then through a room full of roaring machines and unnerving smells. Finally we clamber up two ladders and through two trap doors. The last trap door propels us up and out onto the roof.

London stretches away from us on all sides, vast and densely packed. The often hidden, snaking shape of the river is obvious, with tall buildings that usually seem so sturdy looking like fragile architects' models from this height. Iconic structures look familiar yet totally different viewed from above. Green islands float in the middle of it all and ring the city's outer edges.

This roof isn't designed for people really; it's all aerials, metal girders, pipes, bad smells and huge, noisy fans. Quite a difficult environment to negotiate and definitely not an obvious place from which to watch birds. But actually it's perfect. We've been up here barely ten minutes when we see a peregrine falcon swooping in from the west, over St Paul's Cathedral.

A magnificent hunter that can achieve speeds close to 180mph in the right conditions, this particular one has decided upon a breakfast of feral pigeon. It catches one of London's many in mid-flight and takes it to Tower Bridge – a rather picturesque place to dine and a choice that makes us coo with delight. A telescope is fixed firmly upon its meal making and we all take turns to admire the breakfasting bird. Peregrines catch prey in their talons but it's their vicious beak that delivers the death blow. They then like to pluck their prey before eating it.

Peregrine falcons love the London landscape because it mimics their natural one. They favour cliff faces and mountain crags, and the shapes formed by tall buildings in urban areas are very similar – there are endless manmade ledges that are perfect for nesting and dining. Brought to the brink of extinction across the UK by persecution and pollution, the peregrine falcon is a London success story, and, where there were recently very few, suddenly there are several breeding pairs making a home in the city.

We see a fair few falcons while we're on the roof. We also see a sparrowhawk winging past us to the west, a kestrel, plus numerous gulls and a few swifts. I'm envious of the privileged peace of the world the birds inhabit, gliding on thermals,

blissfully distant from the confusion at ground level. My eyes are mostly drawn southwards, where the landmarks associated with the Thames sit looking tiny, but it's also fun to look north – to find Holloway and pretend I can see the roof winking knowingly at me through the cloudy haze.

Back down on the street and looking upwards to where I've just been, I suddenly feel a little woozy. The bird study group, who are now regularly ascending Tower 42, want the rooftop to become a new kind of nature reserve. It certainly is unique. This was the first time I'd seen peregrines and kestrels in London, though I now realize they are probably constantly soaring above my head, especially when I'm in the centre of town. Who needs rural reserves and escapes to the country, when you can have the world at your feet and raptors dancing around you in the middle of the city?

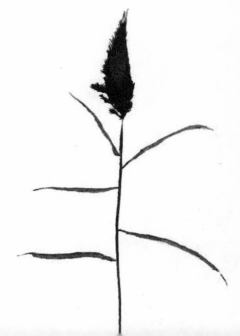

6. Mid May to Mid June

EXCITING TIMES

I'm ridiculously excited. They're currently green and tiny, but I'm anticipating a crop of strawberries in just a few weeks' time. My own glossy red fruit, delicious eaten straight from the hanging basket or perhaps floating in that glass of Pimm's that I've been daydreaming about since March.

The mint is also doing well, its leaves are the brightest of greens and taste delicious. So my plan for cocktails enhanced with home-grown produce is definitely on track. I've been continuing to try to grow cucumbers but this still hasn't worked out. In fact, I planted cucumber seeds and got a crop of mushrooms instead. Odd. They are tall, slender, flawless-looking fungi, but not quite right for adding to drinks. I'm clearly no good at cucumbers but I'm still seriously pleased about the strawberries.

The roof is starting to look a lot greener. Most of the seedlings that started off indoors are flourishing outside full time now. I went away for two weeks at the start of May and when I got back I couldn't believe how alive my tiny little terrace looked. The runner beans have clambered up the side of the house, weaving themselves around the beanpoles and netting I've hung for them. They now also have flowers – orangey red flashes the shape of tiny light bulbs. They look a bit like fairy lights strung on green wire across my white walls. And the tomatoes are getting bigger and more impressive. I replanted a few of them into a grow bag last weekend and they seem happy.

The planting hasn't stopped. I've bought several plugs of evening primroses and tobacco plants for my night area. One of the primroses is making herself at home in an old metal colander, which looks great. I've also sown a few more salad seeds. A plastic trough is now officially an edible leaf box, planted with a newly acquired Provençal salad seed mix, plus some more rocket and basil. With salad you get such satisfyingly instant results – I only planted this trough up a week ago and already it's full of sprouts.

The hot pink planter has proved only a semi-success so far – it's very radish heavy. The 'French Breakfast' radishes, which were planted a couple of months ago, are thriving. The other half of the box, planted with 'Pink Flamingo' beet chard, isn't doing so well. Only one plant has come up after a generous amount of seed was sown. It has gorgeous neon pink highlighted leaves and I'm drowning it in a lot of love and attention, while trying to ignore the failure of the rest of the crop. The planter is also

housing a tall, purple tree spinach plant that has luxuriously vel-
vet looking leaves.

Although I'm leaving the pink plants to develop further before thinking about any sort of harvesting, I am starting to eat
some of my produce now. There's been much fresh coriander
with curry, parsley sprinkled on top of stew and mint leaves
mixed in plain yoghurt. All very tasty.

CITY FARM CRAWL

I've just discovered that London is full of farms – there are sev-
enteen of them, spread all over the city. Armed with this fact and
in need of an adventure, I've employed my most stellar powers
of persuasion and have convinced a friend to accompany me
on an ambitious farm crawl. Our mission is to visit as many
of London's city farms as we can in one day, using only public
transport.

We start our quest out east in the Docklands. Travelling through this sci-fi landscape is like entering another world, one full of sky-scraping steel and glass. It's not a
part of London I spend much time in and I certainly don't
associate it with rural pursuits like horse riding or looking after
livestock.

Our journey begins in Mudchute Park, an idyllic thirty-
two-acre space that includes a farm and equestrian centre. The

weather is glorious, blue skies and sunshine, and at moments it could even be described as hot. It's a short walk to the farm and we're pretty excited by the time we arrive.

All of London's city farms are free entry, and we leisurely amble through, stopping to admire llamas, goats, chickens, ducks and handsome pigs. Horse riders are doing laps of the farm, bathed in soft shafts of romantic summer morning sun and framed by views of the steely Docklands. It's an incongruous but brilliant space – I never imagined I could stand in rolling, sheep-filled fields with Canary Wharf towering in the background.

After a circuit of Mudchute, we jump on a tube to Liverpool Street, emerging in central London around 11.30am. Picking up coffee (for caffeine-addicted me) and chocolate (for my cocoa-addicted friend), we head off towards Spitalfields City Farm, which lies in a housing estate in the middle of Tower Hamlets, one of London's most diverse boroughs but also one of its more deprived. It's a densely built-up spot and the farm offers some welcome tranquillity to the local community. Unlike Mudchute, the focus here is more on growing fruit and veg than keeping livestock, although the farm does have some charming goats and a few other animals.

All sorts of crops are flourishing here, both out in the garden and in the polytunnel. The young farmers' club, made up of kids aged 8-13, is busy tending its produce as we explore the trails that weave around the farm. The growing is imaginative, with a strong emphasis on recycling and lots of enchanting details to look at. I love the barbeque that's been transformed into a container, the hollowed-out gourd pots and the spoons that are now a glinting silver mobile hanging in the eaves of a willow tepee.

After Spitalfields, we eschew trains and use our feet. The walk to Hackney City Farm takes about twenty minutes. Heading in this direction at this time of day is a strategic decision, as this farm is well known for serving a mean lunch in its cafe. But first we wander round the farmyard, encountering some enormous pigs and taking in an attractive walled vegetable garden. The cafe serves up produce from this patch, which is a really wildlife friendly space, and also well labelled so the visitor knows what's what and can steal ideas.

After what turned into a rather long lunch that included lashings of homemade pink lemonade, we walk to Old Street station, take a bus up to Highbury and Islington and walk to Freightliners City Farm, a two-and-a-half-acre site that features an old freight train that's now a plant stall.

The highlights of Freightliners are the bees and the sheep. The bees have their own bee barn and the sheep are the fluffiest you've ever seen. It's impossible not to devote some serious time to stroking them. We enjoy sitting in the yurt at this farm too, as there's something magical about any time spent in a yurt.

Our final stop, Kentish Town City Farm, is north west of

here, so we hop on the Overground train to Gospel Oak and walk from the station, arriving at about 4.30pm. It's sandwiched between three really busy train lines, in a very hectic location. It's London's oldest working farm, with chickens, goats, sheep, cows, horses and some good-looking ducks.

The farm is literally intersected by train tracks and takes its shape from them. The site loops around the train lines so that, at one point, you can be in a field with a cow looking out across the tracks to the goats on the other side, as the cow's lowing blends with the sound of speeding carriages. We watch the cow and its young calf being led back to the barn for the night, apparently unfazed by the rush of transport going on around them.

Despite the trains, the farm is peaceful and we spend a good while in a secluded vegetable patch, trying our hardest to resist some tempting raspberries. Kentish Town City Farm is close to Hampstead Heath and so, after a day's farm crawling, we eventually collapse there on a grassy bank and let the evening roll over us.

Visiting a few farms has got me thinking about urban agriculture more generally. The farms we went to were community spaces, places where people could entertain their kids or while away a couple of rural-feeling hours in the middle of town. They were all producing crops but not enough to feed a city. Should we all be looking to support and implement urban farming on a mass scale? Should London be developing systems of agriculture that mean residents have easy access to relatively cheap, locally grown food and are able to fend for themselves in an age of decreasing food security?

More than half the world's population will be living in urban areas in just a few years' time, while the global population is predicted to be pushing 10 billion by 2050. There simply won't be enough agricultural land to feed all these people, not if they all dare to expect western standards of living. Our global population's demand for food is already putting pressure on rare and important habitats like rainforests. Natural resources that are crucial for wildlife and the health of the planet are increasingly under threat as we continue to rely on food supplies that are produced elsewhere.

Some ambitious and innovative people have been exploring first world urban agriculture in exciting ways. I watched a news report the other day that was about an immense rooftop farm right in the middle of Brooklyn. It's not only producing food for the people nurturing the space but enough to supply local restaurants and food shops as well. Futuristic designs for vertical farms have emerged out of Chicago, a city known for its pioneering approach to creating living roofs and the like. All are very interesting, but actual working examples are rare and most exist purely on paper. Necessity means that cities in the developing world are actually much more advanced when it comes to self-sufficiency. Examples of urban agriculture in places like Havana, Cuba and Dakar, Senegal, to name just two that I know of, are impressive and inspiring.

In London, as well as opportunities to consider constructing bespoke farm buildings and other architectural feats, there's also the potential to be innovative in more low-key ways and to start growing on patches of estranged or forgotten land. Places like schools, hospitals, social housing grounds, parks and other empty sites, or even railway banks and road verges, could all start being used in new ways right now – no complicated engineering required. Near to my house, a disused car park has just been turned into allotments, filled with large raised beds. In a packed out city, we need to be creative about where we plant crops and keep livestock.

On Sunday some friends and I organized a walk around Dalston that was all about re-imagining the cityscape as somewhere with the potential to support more plant life, especially of the edible variety. While wandering the residential streets, we saw loads of examples of people gardening on windowsills, balcony spaces and in front gardens, but we also saw many places that had been smothered in concrete slabs and were devoid of life.

We talked about why it makes sense to grow things and how urban areas are full of spaces that could provide us with delicious greenery, but also how it's easy to become disconnected from the natural world and fearful of getting one's hands dirty; of how it can be hard to care about space that currently looks grim and nobody has a sense of ownership or responsibility for. At the moment I certainly don't feel empowered enough to lay claim to hostile-looking local areas that stand abused and neglected, but I'd like to. We discussed the concept of guerrilla gardening and reclaiming the streets, identifying shared land as we walked – from fenced-off wastelands to the beds around street trees – as places where wildflowers and hardy vegetables could grow. Imagine if each street tree in London had a runner bean twisting around it, communal stalks you could harvest a few fresh beans from on your walk home.

As summer approaches, my roof has already started to turn into a minor jungle, full of tangling vines and the promise of rich harvests to come. London has many tiny jungles like mine and could be home to even more, with all of us trying to grow at least a little of what hits our plates each week. Other cities do it out of necessity already.

For Londoners right now, growing your own is often a hobby, or even a luxury, but it looks like that could change. Western cities' need to cater for themselves is becoming more urgent.

SUMMER

7. Late June into July

There are many adventures to be had in the great outdoors at night. As day colours disperse and dusk rolls in, different shades become more prominent. Our eyes work differently and our ears and noses become more sensitive. Sculptural shadows stretch across lawns and up walls. Pale-leaved plants and white flowers begin to glow in the twilight. Heavy scents grow strong and hang thick in the air, drawing in moths to drink deeply of night nectars.

My after-hours planting has paid off and, when the sun sets, the roof is now lit with luminous petals. The stately tobacco plant is my favourite. Its leaves are sticky, its stalk tall and willowy, and its flowers handsome – fragrant trumpets, star-shaped when you look at them face on, and the brightest of whites. As the light fades, they seem to get ever brighter and whiter. My radish and coriander plants are flowering at the moment too; their flowers are showers of tiny white sparkles that dance around the tobacco trumpets.

Ghostly pollinators of my crops, moths have been the most captivating of dusk visitors. In comparison to their butterfly cousins, moths are unpopular, imagined as drab, dusty, ill-fated creatures attracted to artificial lights and guilty of nibbling clothes, especially the expensive kind. But most species have no interest in cashmere, and many are both inventive and striking. Some of our native species look like tiny birds, with exotic bright feathers and complex markings. The furry elephant hawk moth is bright pink and lime green, the angle shades has wings that look like dead leaves and the buff tip looks like a broken birch twig.

My appreciation of the moth, and my realization that they are anything but boring, came on a summer's evening dedicated to these dusky flyers, when I went to a moth class that took place bang in the middle of King's Cross. There's a tiny nature reserve there, which sits between two mainline stations that connect London with both the north and mainland Europe. Camley Street Natural Park's energy and, at the same time its seclusion, make it a bolt-hole. No matter how many times you find yourself walking its winding paths or staring deeply into its reedy pond, you feel amazed that nature can manage to be so vigorous in such a spot. The fact that it can is exciting and also reassuring. It's a great place to be at night, whether for a spontaneous party or something more worthy, like an ecology class.

We gathered there on a warm evening and set up traps to lure the moths to us. A moth trap is basically a large light, something which is completely irresistible to a moth. The night flyers are baited and hooked on invisible wires, hypnotized and unable to escape the light magnet. They fly in and fall into a container where they can be examined before being set free. The point of moth fishing is to monitor species, to check all is well in their world and establish what kinds of moths are currently flitting around London.

As well as being wowed by bright lights, moths are also drawn in by the fragrant flowers of the likes of tobacco plant, night-scented stocks, evening primrose and soapwort, hence my decision to use some of these plants on my roof. Moths fly all year round but particularly like muggy, moonless nights between April and October. They're not only important pollinators, they're also a valuable food source for other creatures like bats and frogs.

Whenever I've found myself at Camley Street at night, the pond absolutely sings with night-flying insects and draws in bats off the neighbouring Regent's Canal, which is a favoured commuting route for them. A rapid decline in such insects, due to pesticide use and other environmental pressures, has led to a decline in bat numbers. A green space that is rich with insect life can become an attractive after-hours bat feeding ground.

A tiny creature with a huge appetite, the common pipistrelle bat emerges from its summer roost just before sunset and speeds around devouring literally thousands of flying insects. They locate the bugs using high frequency sound waves and eat them on the wing. Inaudible to humans, their call has been variously described as something like a click and a wet slap. Theirs is a fast, jerky flight, zipping around at two to ten metres above the ground. They tend to fly for a couple of hours before returning to their roosting site, but often head out for an extra helping later the same night.

Bats like London's waterways, ponds and parks for feeding, and also enjoy her many buildings, with their wealth of crevices found between roof tiles, eaves and cavity walls, as places of rest. They are known to spend the colder months suspended in Highgate's disused railway tunnels, which have cave-like qualities.

Another bit of green London that is well worth visiting at night is an ancient one way out west. Chelsea Physic Garden was founded in 1673 by the Worshipful Society of Apothecaries, and opens late in the summer so people like me can escape there after work to watch dusk descend with a large glass of wine.

A friend and I accidentally picked an ideal evening to go. The weather was incredible and, once it got dark, we were treated to a garden full of exotic plants (many with magical powers) lit by a full moon. I've never seen as many frogs and toads as I did in the physic garden that night. Each step we took sparked several amphibians into action, with tiny shadowy forms leaping all over the paths and grass. It was brilliant to be in Chelsea, hidden behind high walls in an apothecary's moonlit garden, surrounded by hundreds of jumping toads and frogs. It was like a spell had been cast.

I love the language used to describe the beasts that emerge after dark. 'Nocturnal' means 'of the night', while the term 'vespertine' derives from the Latin *vesper* meaning 'evening (star)' and refers to dusk-loving species. In botanical terms, a vespertine flower blooms exclusively in the evening, while in zoology a vespertine creature is one that's active in the evening, like a bat. My favourite word, though, is 'crepuscular' – it rolls wonderfully around the mouth when you say it out loud. It means 'of twilight' and is used to refer to species that are active in both the early evening and early morning.

Vita Sackville-West's White Garden at Sissinghurst is one of the most famous gardens designed to be experienced after sunset. 'Much have I loved the night', she wrote, 'drinking the deep nocturnal silences . . . only with nightfall could I stand apart and view the shaping pattern of my way'.

It's the weekend of the summer solstice, when daylight hours are at their longest. It's getting late but it's still just about light. I'm not long back from a production of Julius Caesar and I've been finding watering the plants a soothing antidote to all the tragedy of the last few hours. As a dusk duvet wraps itself around the roof, giving the plants some love is sweet relief after a Shakespearean bloodbath. I've just discovered my first rooftop caterpillar perched on Edith the rose, a miniature ex-houseplant named after my flatmate's grandmother. The caterpillar is brilliant green and looks fluorescent against Edith's pink petals in the half-light.

So much has changed on the roof in the last month. It's all berries, beans and bees at the moment. Well, to be honest the berries are no more, I've already eaten them all. The tiny green strawberries swelled and turned red and have been duly devoured. They tasted sweet and tangy and just extra special because I'd grown them myself. As predicted, my hanging basket did look gorgeous dripping with ripe berry baubles.

The plan was to save a few to take to the tennis at Wimbledon next week but I failed to exercise enough self-control. It is simply impossible to ignore a strawberry when it is calling to you from your balcony. Once you've eaten one you're doomed. You'll be pleased to learn that I was a good gardener and did manage to share. It was a small crop so now I'm feeding the plants up, hoping desperately for more fruit later this summer.

I do still have beans though, and they're getting bigger by the minute. Tomorrow a friend is coming over for a solstice supper and we will eat the first harvest, toasted with potent drinks full of crushed home-grown mint. I love my runner beans – I love the fact I can remember so clearly buying their seeds on a snowy day by the sea, that they shared my room for weeks, and that they're now a thick tumble of leaves, flowers and vegetables growing against our exterior bathroom wall. I have become a boastful mother and am brimming with pride.

I've had many bumblebee visitors, plus less furry kinds of bee as well. In return for my best and sweetest nectar, they've been efficiently pollinating my crops. It's official – bees love runner beans, just like me. My beans have proved incredibly easy to grow, creating a satisfyingly fast mass of vegetation in the smallest of places.

I ate my first radish recently. It took a while for me to persuade myself to do it as I battled with a bizarre guilt about eating something I'd spent so long growing. For some reason I wasn't sure I would be able to grow anything as exotic as a radish and was faintly suspicious it would taste funny. It is with relief that I report that it tasted just as a radish should, cool then hot – a crunchy, peppery, magical root. I've discovered that radishes are easy to grow in containers and their flowers are terribly pretty. I think it's actually bad gardening practice to let radishes flower or bolt, but I can't help myself.

The tomatoes are doing well, getting stronger and sturdier. Today I spotted the first flowers budding on one of the plants. I cannot wait for them to fruit. They're going to taste so good with my rocket, which is also doing well and has been a favourite with most meals over the last two weeks. I've taken to mixing freshly picked mint, rocket, coriander and parsley leaves into fromage frais, as a cooling side to hot dishes.

It's dark out on the roof now, the shortest night of the year has begun and the moths are on the move. It's been hot of late so I've been sleeping with the door open, with rooftop breezes blowing gently around my bedroom, my dreams wafted with roof dew and birdsong (and, OK, wailing sirens and the drone of helicopters). It's lovely, noisiness included.

8. August

As a faintly impoverished twenty-something in rented accommodation, it can be a challenge to be a grower. It's the challenge that makes it interesting though, that 'against the odds' element and the fact it's perhaps slightly surprising even to try. What I love most about London is its endless capacity to surprise. With my new interest in growing has come the discovery that I'm not alone, that lots of city dwellers are getting inventive with out-of-the-ordinary spaces. My gardening ambitions don't make me original at all.

I have new eyes now I'm officially an urban gardener, eyes that are attracted to pots balancing precariously on ledges and that see all spare spaces as a potential flower bed or vegetable patch. London is absolutely full of green spaces. There are the glorious parks, but there are also hundreds of smaller scale, more secret gardens that one can seek out – community gardens, allotments, local nature reserves and borough growing projects.

I had a little adventure in Hackney last week with a woman called Hedvig. Get Growing is a project she runs that's giving people who sign up the equipment, guidance and moral support to start growing vegetables in their outside space, whatever shape or size it may be. They're working with ten households this season whose growing spaces range from window boxes and roof terraces to front steps and backyards. The people involved are either novices or gardeners who've become disheartened due to a lack of success.

Get Growing teaches the principles of permaculture and gives people one-on-one, practical tuition. The enthusiasm surrounding the project is infectious. When discussing it, Hedvig glowed with the sheer joy of sharing growing know-how and watching people who've signed up become confident gardeners. It functions as a community building scheme too – they've also linked up with various local projects, all devoted to urban growing and outreach work.

We cycled to one of the Get Growing gardens – a front

yard that's a ten-minute ride from Hedvig's own house. She'd been there earlier in the day, delivering compost using a bike trailer.

Hedvig didn't know it, but I'd never cycled in London before. I was a city cycling virgin, but that day I suddenly found myself on a bike. I loved it. I even survived being overtaken by an eighteen-metre-long bendy bus without emitting even the smallest of squeals. My bicycle bravery was rewarded with a tour of a garden that's the work of a lady called Joanne.

Joanne's front garden and front steps are dripping with veg. She has beans, courgettes, aubergines, strawberries, tomatoes, herbs and salad. Neighbours have started calling out compliments from across the street. She plans to install a wormery and a compost bin next. Suddenly she has found her street is a much friendlier place and she's bubbling with confidence. Hedvig seemed very proud. Gardening can be such a powerful force for good. It's even managed, in a roundabout way, to convince me to get a bike. Carting compost home from the garden centre a few days later by bus, I dreamed of having a trailer like Hedvig's.

I've stumbled upon various quirky growing projects this year. Peering through a fence in King's Cross, I see that several skips, or drop boxes, have been planted with vegetables. Daydreaming on Waterloo Bridge, my attention is caught by a scrap of land where supermarket trolleys have become planters. In Deptford, south east London, some trolleys retrieved from the Thames are now creek-side plant containers too.

Turns out everyone's at it. One of my best friends has just moved to west London after spending most of her post university years on the road, most recently in Africa. In need of an adventure and her own little bit of wilderness, she's taken to climbing out of her bedroom window and has been gradually turning the flat roof of her house into a plant nursery. This summer she's successfully growing everything from aubergines to squash out there, though apparently the cabbages have been a disaster.

Another friend has created a heaving tomato plantation in a glass laundry room down in south London, while one in a Camden flat, with no outside space but lots of windowsills, tells me he's been growing strawberries. Another has a gorgeous, floating deck-top garden aboard her boat on the river, which sits in the wake of Tower Bridge and has fine views out to Greenwich. London is a city of growers, who are nurturing land in all kinds of peculiar spaces.

THE FOREST EDGE

I'm now the proud owner of a handsome bronze bike from the seventies and I've named her Hedvig in honour of the lady who got me cycling. Today I rode all the way to Chingford, which is practically in Essex. I cycled along the River Lea, a neat band of water flowing through a landscape that's a mixture of marshland and light industry.

Swans glided through glassy water that was rimmed with tall reeds and rippled with the reflections of warehouses, pylons and waste processing plants. Cranes framed the river edges. Mallard ducklings bobbed alongside the odd rusting can and billowing plastic bag. Butterflies danced, the sun shone, geese nibbled at the cycle path. Colourful graffiti decorated river walls and a board announced that the river is so healthy now that otters are known to be using it. The ride was a long one; it took about an hour, but I did it at a leisurely pace with a new friend. The path was quiet, especially as we got further east towards Epping Forest.

Our destination was a place called Hawkwood, a food grow-ing project set in scenic grounds on the edges of London and the edges of the forest. The air there echoes with the hammer-ing of woodpeckers. Amazingly, we could hear no traffic. The site was once a tree and flower nursery, supplying local parks with plant life. It ran out of money and stood empty for years, before a group of organic gardeners took over the site and set up a food growing co-operative. The project is a young one but the people are full of energy and ambition. They sell their produce at a local market and run a veg box scheme. They have fund-ing for three years but want to be self-financing and independ-ently run soon. A range of permaculture courses are planned to spread the gardening bug throughout the borough of Waltham Forest and beyond. It's all very inspiring.

In the morning, they set me to work in the warm glasshouse, nurturing climbing cucumbers that are proving a lot more successful than my own elusive crop. After a long lunch, I was outside getting a bit more physical, hammering old scaffold planks into bed shapes and hauling compost and straw. The conversation was good and the weather fine. On the long ride home, my legs ached from all the exertion and I barely made it up a steep hill near home, but I felt great. The water ran a muddy brown when I showered back at the flat. Post wash, I felt refreshed but also exhausted in the way you only do when you've been out all day, breathing fresh air and flexing muscles and limbs that are normally fairly sedentary.

COURAGE AND CREATIVITY

I've developed some strange habits since acquiring the roof. I garden first thing on Saturday mornings, slightly hungover, contact lens-less, hair wild and pyjama clad. I make my best gardening decisions in this state. I find I'm suddenly brave enough to prune back the tomatoes, no longer shy about lopping off the thick foliage that's casting them in shade. And suddenly my brain can process the creative string work required to get my wild runner beans in order.

So yes, I've been doing some emergency repairs on the roof. My beans have grown so big and bushy that they've become quite unwieldy and are prone to collapse. Their netting and canes, which seemed such sturdy support when they were young, are struggling to keep them in order these days. They look wonderful, a wild tangle of green vines, but they're causing a certain amount of havoc, especially when the wind picks up. In terms of bean control, I've been inventive with a ball of string and I'm hoping they're now secure. I ate some beans with my dinner yesterday evening, young, tender ones. They were delicious, which was a relief. I served up a rather stringy number to a friend at the weekend, which was a little embarrassing. I've learned my lesson – don't try and impress people with king size beans. The small ones taste far better, even if they look slightly pathetic.

The best news from the roof at the moment is that I have lots of tomatoes. The plants are looking healthy and strong, covered in flowers and tiny fruits that I'm rapt watching grow bigger and plumper by the day. Some are round and some are plum-shaped. My labelling system turned out not to be weather resistant so I'm now unsure of which variety is which, but I don't think that really matters, as long as they taste good.

I can't wait for them to start turning red. My thoughts are currently dominated by fresh, just picked tomatoes, sliced and topped with fresh, just-picked basil or fresh, just-picked rocket. Summer salad heaven, right here on my roof, a short crawl from bed. I imagine I'll soon be breakfasting on sun-warmed tomatoes straight from the vine while still in sleepwear. Like the beans before them, having known the tomatoes when they were the tiniest of seeds makes seeing them bloom and fruit all the more exciting.

I'm enjoying the salad leaves I've been growing, eating them almost daily and really delighting in how many different and intense flavours a simple leaf can offer. I'm also enjoying the process of picking, there's something tranquil about five minutes spent harvesting leaves for supper. It's a good time for calm thoughts.

The roof has looked at its prettiest florally over the last few weeks. The flowering tobacco has been joined by yellow evening primroses, prongs of purple lavender and deep orange nasturtiums. I recently inherited a courgette plant that has five fluorescent flowers now. All these blooms mean I continue to have frequent bee visitors. They've been welcome company, seeming to most like drinking from the lavender when I'm curled up next to it with a book. And today I had my first butterfly. I lost a good fifteen minutes stalking it round the roof trying to get a photograph, but it wasn't having any of it. After being thoroughly harassed by a girl wielding a camera, flapping as manically as it was in the end, it fluttered off over the chimney tops, leaving me picture-less.

Among the plants I most definitely planted, from seed or

seedling, there are some rogue growths that have appeared from nowhere. There's a plant with the smallest, prettiest purple flowers that's growing in a old green ceramic pot that, as far as I was concerned, contained nothing but a little bit of old, crumbly compost. There's also something more recognizable as some kind of dandelion-type-thing growing in an old basket. I looked this one up. I was hoping it was nipplewort but I think it's some kind of hawkweed, a great but perhaps not quite so amusing name.

In the same basket, the statuesque purple tree spinach continues to grow. The spinach is a funny one, as I thought I'd planted chard. I think the squirrels must have transplanted it. Despite the missing chard – an apparently easy leaf that I'm proving incapable of growing – I'm pleased with the spinach. It has matte leaves that look like they've been dipped in an intense purple powder, and I like its tall, elegant and slender look.

BEACH COMBING

The Thames has let out a long breath, slimming down to half its size. The sun beats the water to dark silver, a ribbon folded in on itself. It has retreated to leave mud like silk, pooled with wet shadows, and a beach of broken brick, pot and stone. Our window has arrived. We have just an hour for beach combing, for some concentrated overturning of rock and masonry.

This is new terrain for me, whose feet are more used to asphalt and carpet. This earth moves underfoot, invites me in and sucks around my soles, staining them a rich, fertile grey. And the ground further off is made of discarded shells, like so many empty houses awaiting demolition, an unrefined sand that crunches deliciously underfoot.

I stand still in this freshly exposed landscape and my eyes cast out over the river. Gulls settle on floating platforms, geese bob, a heron hunts on the water's edge. Tracing the lips of the far shore, a white parasol weaves through dark green. The trees seem darker because the sun is in our eyes and the lady with the umbrella seems all the whiter, like a ghost, you say, or driftwood.

We walk, we chatter and we all try and claim a bit of this for ourselves, a quiet moment apart. I crouch down in the damp and push my fingers into cool silt. Turning over river-worn bricks and smooth stones, London reveals yet more of herself. In the swarming life of a beach made from smashed up history lessons, I see the smallest creatures homemaking in Roman ruins, cosying up in rusting industrial leftovers, making a life among fragments of Victorian tea sets and broken IKEA dinner plates.

One rock attracts my attention, printed like fabric with

crisp dots, the pattern made by the baked tracks of sundried leeches. Live ones shrink and grow, mirroring the movement of their tidal river habitat. The leeches glisten on the underbelly of old masonry alongside tiny, almost transparent shrimp. Hundreds of them are indignant at my interruption.

I move on and am drawn to the swampy islands that have emerged, with patterns woven into their sides by the water and all who live there. Textures that demand to be touched. Visiting mitten crabs have constructed fairy tale grottoes in the slippery mud banks, all hung over with weed, reed and willow.

In the shallow ponds gathered at our feet, fish course. Nets sweep through the water, unearthing unsuspecting species. Alert to our explorations, flounders disguise themselves. They are our native chameleons, able to disappear into the gravel on the river's bed. A veteran of the water's harsher ways, a sea-worn crab, missing a pincer and a leg, is plucked out and into a study tray. Another, a mere youth, has a newly formed shell that is springy and soft to the touch.

Our hour's up. We leave the shrinking shore and walk back up the steps, to streets braced for flood. The river draws in its breath, rises and spreads, loosens and shakes out its hair for the evening ahead. The sky softens, turns the water orange, and the river's flow grows stronger in its course east to meet the sea.

THE ELUSIVE EEL

I've sadly never seen one, but the elusive European eel is strongly associated with London's rivers. Any Cockney will be familiar with the jellied eel, once common fare, now perhaps more of an East End delicacy or even a culinary dare. The eel is one of the Thames' most interesting and enigmatic species. Long-lived and multicoloured, this sometime Londoner originates from the saltier climes of the Sargasso Sea, to which it returns when it's ready to breed.

The leaf-shaped larvae, or *leptocephali*, ride on the currents of the Gulf Stream and North Atlantic Drift towards Europe and North Africa. When they reach European shores, they metamorphose into transparent glass eels. As they move further inshore, and ride the tides up estuaries and tidal rivers, the freshwater mix triggers pigmentation. At this stage they are called elvers.

An eel will live in this environment for many years, hugging the coastline of estuaries or moving into freshwater, where they turn a yellow colour, gain body weight and grow in length. As an eel reaches maturity, its eyes become bigger, its head broader, fat content increases and the undersides of its skin start to shine silver or bronze.

Eventually the slippery silver eel will make its way downriver and back to its breeding grounds. Not much is known about its

North Atlantic migration, but once back in the Sargasso Sea, it lives in mud, crevices and under stones. Spawning occurs during winter and early spring.

Since the seventies, the number of eels reaching Europe is thought to have declined by around 90 percent. Potential causes include over-fishing, spread of parasites, river barriers such as hydroelectric plants, and natural changes in the North Atlantic Oscillation, Gulf Stream and the North Atlantic Drift. PCB (polychlorinated biphenyl) pollution is probably another big reason for their decline. The best time to spot eels in London is apparently in late June and early July. Scientists are trying to learn more about this threatened species, and traps in Thames' tributaries are being used to monitor numbers passing through.

9. Mid August into September

I wasn't completely convinced it would happen, but the tomatoes are gradually blushing and turning from yellow to orange to ripe red. I can't tell you how proud I am to be responsible for such a seriously healthy crop of fruit grown by my own hands, from seed no less. I know I'm being sentimental, nostalgic and possibly a little ridiculous, but it really does feel funny to think back to the little seedlings that shared my bedroom in early spring and to look at what they've now become. They taste wonderful by the way, in the way only home-grown tomatoes do.

They've been a demanding bunch over the last month though, requiring much attention from my watering can and fainting dramatically if I dare to neglect them during a hot spell. The roof has been looking a little frazzled of late. We've had some biblical downpours here but a lot of the pots are quite sheltered and sometimes they need watering even when it's rained.

I do like watering, there's an almost meditative quality to it, but, after a long day in the office followed by a late night, I admit it can be a struggle to satiate the plants' thirst. It's been the main job on the roof recently, that and keeping the beans and tomatoes under control. Both have grown huge, so I've had to do lots of trimming and tying back.

My flat is truly tiny and having the roof doubles the size of my bedroom. I often find myself out there late or first thing in the morning, and, if it's dry and I'm home, I always eat out there. It's a busy spot, watched over by many windows, under several flight paths and buffeted by noise from the roads and various house parties, but it's still my most peaceful place.

It's from here I can quietly spy on foxes running between houses and admire dewdrops sparkling on spiders' webs. It's here I feel most at home and most at one with the city, like I've staked a claim to my own small spot and that I'm also part of a wider city system. I like being alone here, long solitary afternoons and evenings on my perch are ones well spent. But it's good to share and the roof has become the living room I intended, expanding my minuscule flat beyond its four walls and providing space for me to welcome friends. It's somewhere for lazy weekend coffees, for cakes and bubbling romance. It's also the place where I can best show off the fruits of my gardening labours.

The home-grown meal, eaten in the very place where it was nurtured, is one of the most satisfying suppers you can have. People are always impressed by your green-fingered prowess, removing the need to be a brilliant cook. I treat a couple of university friends to dinner on the roof. There's lots of food, including fresh salad straight from the flower pot, just picked beans lightly steamed, tomatoes still warm from a day in the sun and, most importantly, there's drinking. Large jugs of boozy punch, flavoured with leaves from the garden. How fine fresh mint is on such an occasion. We eat, drink and play a highly competitive game of Scrabble as the evening darkens and descends into absolute silliness.

RADICAL NATURE

I spent Sunday afternoon at Dalston Mill, a temporary installation on a patch of wasteland in east London, which is part of a Radical Nature exhibition that's currently on. The mill sits on a wedge of land behind the busy Dalston Junction Interchange, between a crumbling disused building, a garage and a shopping centre car park. The area has been taken over by a collective of architects and environmentalists who have transformed it into a working windmill and wheat field, with a performance space. My friend and I had only planned to spend an hour there but we somehow spent four, persuaded to take part in various workshops and just generally being charmed by a space that has found new life for a few weeks as a community garden.

The idea is to break bread with anyone who enters the space, bread made with freshly milled flour and baked on site. The wheat looks stunning, ripe and gold, stretching out like a sandy beach and brushing against the graffiti-sprayed brick walls of the neighbouring buildings. The temporariness of the site and the project, and the speed with which it was conceived, realized and with which it will be dismantled, is what gives it its energy. It's fantastic to be able to access one of those mysterious yet numerous patches of disused land that exist all over London and probably every city, to be able to explore its undergrowth and realize its massive potential.

I also went to see the wider Radical Nature exhibition, which looks at the experimental art and architecture that's emerged out of land art, environmental activism and utopianism since 1969. Nature has provided creative inspiration for centuries, but the exhibition curators argue that, since the sixties, the increasingly evident degradation of the natural world has brought a new urgency to artists' and architects' responses to our changing world. I loved the idea but found the show itself slightly disappointing.

A Richard Long retrospective at Tate Britain, by contrast, was pure brilliance and something of a revelation to me. As someone who had never really explored the idea of land art before, Long's rock sculptures and poetically brief word pictures of walks blew me away. More art exhibitions linked to environmentalism and the natural world are planned for other major London spaces later this year and beyond. It seems to be a popular theme at the moment, probably because so many of us are discovering our inner environmentalist and want to react in some way, whether by creating or visiting something that reflects our ecological concerns.

SCORCHED LANDSCAPE

I adore hot weather. All good intentions of reading or studying or doing something vaguely useful disappear on sunny days and I just sink into a rooftop seat and sun doze for hours. Although I am capable of being extremely lazy, I have also had the urge to explore of late, to walk through the somewhat scorched London landscape and find places where the grass is long and the insects are busy.

Happily there is one such place right by my house, a fifteen-minute stroll towards Arsenal. It's an area with an enormous football ground, several train lines and a nature reserve called Gillespie Park, which runs along the railway and offers fine views of the looming stadium and the identikit blocks of flats built in its wake.

I walk along the insanely busy Seven Sisters Road. Reaching the station at Finsbury Park, I disappear through a discreet metal gate, up some steps and into the long, bleached grass I've been craving. There are hundreds of yellow and purple wildflowers, and many bees and butterflies. I've come on a workday, taken some time off, and so the park is almost all mine; very few people are about. I walk through the small reserve for hours, photographing details and trying to film insects (which I fail miserably at). Trains speed past throughout but somehow the noise is negligible. I forget it, too taken with the vegetation, with the way that some plants reach my armpits and how the sun is beating far-off objects into silhouette. The sky is full of haze and rippling with heat.

It's important that former wastelands like this one, bordering railways and dense areas of housing, can be transformed into such islands of wildness. The windmill, wheat field and garden in Dalston are all brilliantly creative, but, while their temporariness gives them a vigour and pace that you don't find at Gillespie, that temporariness is ultimately frustrating. What's great about this park is how established it's starting to feel, how permanent. This random greenery is as much a part of the character of London as any grand monument, and it should be valued and protected just as much.

It really is incredibly hot in the city at the moment. The Evening Standard billboards declared that it reached 41 degrees yesterday. In need of a long lunch away from the sweaty misery of our desks, a work friend and I decided to walk across the river and up the Monument, a sixty-two-metre-high column built in the 1670s to commemorate the great fire of London. We climbed to the top and watched London shimmer and warp in her heat bubble.

The tower is quite modest height-wise nowadays; you can get more panoramic views from other London buildings, but the Monument view is interesting for the details you get – the emergency escapes from office blocks, air conditioning units, blank grey space.

Imagine if all these companies made gardens of their rooftops. Heat waves like this one would seem a lot less severe – the heat island effect created by endless concrete would be reduced by living surfaces. It would look stunning too. London has got a few living roofs, aerial spaces that are literally alive, not just with pots and planters like mine, but entire rooftops that are covered in layers of earth, or substrate, where plants can grow roots and wildlife can make a more permanent home. But there definitely could be many more; parts of the city are oppressively grey. There are vast areas of aggressive steel and brick where you'd be forgiven for forgetting that there was any life on earth other than of the human variety.

TOWN AND COUNTRY

I've just returned from a wedding out in the country. My friends married under an ancient oak tree with flowers in their hair, and we toasted them in an orchard with local cider dyed pink with blackberry juice. We feasted in a yurt decorated with homemade bunting and watched a band play in an old hay barn. Butterflies danced endlessly and such stars shone when night fell. Now I'm back in London, in busy air that seethes and rushes.

I can't imagine happiness that didn't somehow involve the city but sometimes my life of concrete and glass makes me feel a little sad. Mournful, I take to listening to folk songs about remote lakes and knotty pines, as my feet beat a path over unforgiving tarmac. I walk with tear-studded eyes that blur ever-burning streetlights into blazing streams. At moments like these it's essential to seek out the city's wilds and escape to her secret, camouflaged places.

Summer draws to an end with an adventure on another Londoner's roof. Temporary pop-up shops and supper clubs have been all the rage in town this summer and a friend and I are heading to a pop-up-restaurant-cum-fairytale-installation in an artist's east London home. The artist in question has a live/work space that he's transformed into a fantastical culinary venue. A few of us stay late on the final Sunday of the project and are lucky enough to get to explore his large roof.

We climb a ladder and discover a wondrous aerial space that's complete with a bedroom that is a cross between a turret and a garden shed, and a spacious chicken run, with three birds pecking happily about. It's great to see them here, calm and cool despite being faced with the hectic carnival of a big night out in a grimy part of town.

Keeping chickens on a roof is an imaginative thing to do. It speaks of the endless possibilities of random urban spaces. Nature, in whatever form, somehow feels more important in places such as these. It's beautiful here, unconventionally so, but beautiful nonetheless.

Back on my own roof, after battling with temptation, I've come to terms with the fact that I can't get chickens of my own, as my space is tiny in comparison to the artist's. The rooftop really has turned into a little jungle over the last few months though. I've been looking back at photographs I took of it in March and the difference between then and now is dramatic. The roof has looked so alive in the last few weeks.

As we've crept into September, it's probably passed from its most verdant stage to looking a little rough round the edges. Most of the flowers have gone to seed now, the strawberries are in need of attention and salad leaves are sparser. Crumpled bean leaves blow into my room, hinting at autumn. They do still have flowers though, so my bean suppers are safe yet.

I've started thinking a little about winter crops and developing a kind of cold weather plan. Reluctantly in part, as I'd like to pretend summer will last forever, but also with some excitement. Winter will be a happier season if it involves growing or at least nurturing crops. I've been reading about hardy lettuces that you sow over winter to harvest in early spring. Books also suggest sowing Japanese and spring onions, winter spinach, turnips and Chinese greens in late summer, and planting garlic and daffodil bulbs in early autumn.

But for now there's actually still lots left to eat – beans, herbs, salad, maybe a courgette if I'm lucky, a new chilli plant, plus all these tomatoes. I intend to make the most of the warm weather and still light-ish evenings for a good while yet.

AUTUMN

10. Late September into October

I had the unexpected pleasure of meeting two older ladies the other day, Daphne and Lillian, who've called an imposing Hackney tower block home for over thirty years. I spent a bright autumnal morning listening to them rave about the natural spectacles they witness from their cloud-capped building. The pair sit contentedly in the kitchen of their seventh-floor flat, drinking tea and chain-smoking cigarettes, admiring a sweeping view out over a reservoir and beyond to central London.

A guest in their smoky kitchen, my eyes traced the shapes of the Gherkin, BT Tower and the London Eye in the distance, before settling closer to home on the steeple of a local church and then on the many birds resting on the glittering water at the tower block's feet. I listened to the ladies' wild tales of foxes and electric storms, and had my eyes opened. A grim-looking building, which on the surface spoke of the worst kind of bleak, packed urban living, was actually airy and light inside, boasted the most magnificent views of both nature and the city, and was the home of two engaging women.

A few days later I found myself in central London, lying on the grass in St James's Park, staring at a sky framed by the yellowing leaves of London plane trees. Later, cycling along Regent's Canal, I admired a Virginia creeper that was turning a deep, glossy red as it crept across the side of a brick warehouse.

Autumn is certainly in the air, although there are still summery moments to be had on the roof. Even now, I can be found out there in my shorts, indulging in some last-minute sunbathing. But yes, a change of season is definitely imminent. There's a horse chestnut tree at the end of my street dropping conkers all over the place, and the local squirrel community suddenly seems a lot more active again, busy burying treats in preparation for harsh weather ahead.

One grey squirrel has started experimenting with tomatoes. My tomatoes. My lovingly nurtured-from-seed tomatoes. I'm not a bad person, I'm willing to share, but this squirrel doesn't even like tomatoes. He steals one (often a barely ripe specimen), eats half, then leaves the remains in a pulpy mess in a flower pot. He doesn't learn. The next day he'll take another, eat half, realize it's not the fruit for him, and discard the rest. I'm sure you can appreciate that this is most annoying. It really wouldn't be so bad if he ate the whole thing and enjoyed it.

They are marvellous, the tomatoes. I'm picking a few every

day now, eating some straight off the vine, dropping some into salads and filling little tubs with them to take to work. A little box of tomatoes makes my computer-bound desk job almost bearable. I'm expecting to be harvesting them for a while yet.

The beans, sadly, aren't faring so well and are actually in a bit of a state at the moment. They're looking elderly and wizened, with bald patches and browning leaves. They're also home to some mysterious bugs – bugs that look like a cross between a ladybird and a beetle, and like hanging out in large gangs on runner beans. I'm not sure if they're responsible for the beans' demise, or whether it's old age that's got to them.

I do feel sad that they're dying, but we had a good summer together. I've had some absolutely delicious bean suppers – they've tasted best simply steamed – and I've also managed to impress a few people with them. I took a bundle to a potluck dinner party a few weeks ago and they proved popular. Bean compliments are a pleasure to receive.

I've been making preparations to extend the growing season on the roof, seeking out crops that are hardy enough to survive a deep chill. I've planted spring onions for early next year, and chard, spinach, parsley and rocket that I hope to harvest during autumn and the milder part of winter. I'm going to plant garlic and investigate perhaps planting some winter brassicas. I also bought some spring bulbs this weekend, the classic daffodils and crocuses, and a couple of giant alliums.

The other thing I've been doing more of as October approaches is seed collecting. The seeds that are drying in my room at the moment look ornamental, stuffed in an old glass bottle and sitting on a low coffee table fashioned out of a cardboard box and disguised with a rug. The ballooning radish seedpods and the umbrella-like coriander seeds look particularly nice; the coriander ones are quite tempting to nibble on now and then.

VISITATIONS

October's arrived and the weather is warm and windy. Whipped up leaves are dropping everywhere. Despite gloomy skies, walking along the tree-lined Southbank yesterday was like walking through a golden riverside forest, yellowed plane tree leaves tumbling all over the place, softening the pavement and painting it with autumn. It's always fun to walk through just fallen foliage.

Today it's bright, sunny and blustery, good conditions for the fair weather gardener, and I've finally finished my winter prep. The beans came down last weekend. I did battle with tough vines that were tangled with netting and bamboo sticks for about an hour. And so today, the large pots that housed the runners over summer have been freshly dug and planted with flower and garlic bulbs. The netting and sticks have become a complicated squirrel deterrent system, which I fear probably won't work.

Despite being a good for nothing gardener if the weather isn't up to scratch, I have been managing to enjoy the roof as things get cooler and wetter. I've actually more than tolerated recent rain, as I've seen the plants appreciate getting a good soaking. And the roof's actually looking really pretty at the moment, crispy and crunchy, but also colourful.

Months on, my tobacco plants are still flowering and I've had some surprise late evening primrose blooms. My heather is dazzling with its purple blossoms, while the lavender flowers have dried to a crumbly grey and are very smelly. I'm going to use its sprigs to perfume my room. Even my basil plant has been sporting delicate white flowers this month. The roof's less of a jungle these days but it's definitely still jungle-ish.

One sign of a thriving garden is the creatures that visit. October has seen not just the usual wood pigeons and squirrels doing acrobatics in the sycamore tree, but also a black, white and red great spotted woodpecker. I knew woodpeckers lived in London, but I'd never actually seen one. It was a thrilling moment when I peered out of our steamy bathroom window, over the roof and into the tree, and saw it tap tap tapping at the sycamore's trunk.

Colour- and-marking wise, the woodpecker has a lot in common with the mystery bugs that are living on the roof. Made temporarily homeless by the felling of the runner beans, they've relocated to various other spots. I've learned they are the mid instar nymphs of the southern green shield bug (*Nezara viridula*), a newcomer to UK shores. A native of Africa, they get accidentally imported over here, hiding in food deliveries. They're common in southern parts of Europe and are becoming more common here too, apparently being big fans of tomatoes and beans. No wonder they're attracted to my warm, bean- and tomato-filled roof.

Doing a little more research, I've found out that the no longer mystery bugs do damage crops like beans, causing loss of blooms, leaves and distorted fruit. Mystery solved and also very interesting. Maybe this is an indicator species of how our climate is changing and the effect such changes are having on both wildlife and food crops. As the weather gets warmer and wetter, different creatures will be able to live here, but others, that favour cooler temperatures, will be pushed further north. Climate change is going to have a massive impact on wildlife, and climatic alterations mean there are exotic new pests for gardeners to contend with.

Leaving bug worries behind, I'm still harvesting tomatoes as autumn advances. I just popped out and picked one in fact and it was as delicious as ever. Things are slowing down though; it's taking a lot longer for them to go red. I'm attempting to ripen a few picked green ones inside now. A ripe, red tomato is being used to coax a bowl of green ones to blush. It's working but it's a slow process. I'm practising patience and savouring them one by one as they turn. Last weekend I planted more winter lettuce, and the hardy salads and leaves I planted in September are doing well, sending up lots of green shoots. I think the roof will keep providing for a while yet.

11. Late October into November

I've just discovered a new park – it's long and thin and really near where I live. The New River Walk follows the course of the manmade New River, which once brought water to Sadler's Wells from springs in Hertfordshire, north of London. Much of the London stretch of the river is now underground but an overground section gives shape to a park that winds its way from Highbury down to Angel.

I wandered along it on a late October afternoon. Weeping willows cast the silvery, green water in shifting shade, bushes were studded with berries and trees flashed with red, orange, brown and pink. Ducks cut trails through pond weed that was slicked thickly over the water. And people walked – in couples, with kids, with dogs, alone. All was deeply autumnal and picturesque.

After said walk, I took a train to Brighton, where a university friend is now living. She's volunteering on an allotment that sits on top of a steep hill above the seaside city. The rolling one-acre plot has gorgeous views – Brighton and the sea in one direction, the South Downs stretching out in the other. We spent a couple of hours up there that weekend, picking snails off cabbages and harvesting rocket and late raspberries.

The best job by far, though, was apple pressing. The allotment holders had borrowed a traditional press and were on a mission that weekend to juice as many apples as possible to turn into cider. Using the chopping machine was really satisfying. We used it to crush the apples into pulp by grinding them through a vicious set of teeth. I got plastered in skins and juice as I chopped.

The allotment produces a large amount of food that's shared between the people that work on it. I took a big bag of rocket back to London with me, which lasted for almost a week. In comparison to the roof, the productivity levels there are immense and I'm slightly in awe of it. My rooftop yield seems fairly meagre in comparison.

Talking of apples, I've been daydreaming about my mother's homemade apple and blackberry pie recently, an ample wedge of it drowning in thick, piping hot custard. Mum's pie tastes especially good because her crumbly pastry wraps home-grown apples, sweetened and stained with blackberries foraged from the hedgerows near her house.

My pie-shaped reveries have got me thinking about orchards

and how valuable they can be. Traditional orchards often contain a mosaic of habitats – a range of trees, scrub, hedgerows and grasslands – that can support much wildlife. Autumn sees creatures feasting on fallen fruit and fruit-loving insects, in preparation for the cold months ahead. Mistletoe is spread by the mistle thrush and is semi-parasitic, mostly on apple trees. Strung about in orchards, its white berries are a great source of food for birds during winter. Fungi like waxcaps, giant puffballs and field mushrooms emerge on the orchard floor, while bracket fungus extends from the tree trunks.

Living in London, I thought perhaps there wouldn't be that many orchards about. I was completely wrong, of course. A quick search revealed there are loads of orchards here, some hundreds of years old, others brand new community projects. I work just south of the river and it turns out this area has a connection with an apple variety called the Cellini – 'a fine, showy and handsome apple', according to *The Fruit Manual*, published in 1884. It was raised by nurseryman Leonard Phillips of Vauxhall and introduced in 1828, then grown around London throughout the nineteenth century.

I'm not sure my roof could ever support fruit trees, but apple-shaped thoughts have led to my meeting and helping some inspiring Londoners plant fruit trees around a nearby low-rise housing estate. Locals have transformed their communal green space into an orchard that will soon be heavy with apples, pears, plums and even mulberries for years to come.

Perhaps not the most obvious thing to actively seek out, orchards are also fantastic places for some serious moss and lichen spotting. If you adjust your eyes to the more micro side of life, lichens dye the landscape a rainbow of colours, while miniature forests and mountains of moss gleam with wet. When I was little I used to spend hours making up stories about the people who lived in the tiny worlds of moss and lichen.

Lichens come in four forms – the crustose types; the brilliantly named squamulose types; the foliose types (that are sometimes jelly-like); and the frutiose types (that are almost hairy to look at). Lichens are dual organisms made up of two different life forms that exist in a harmonious, symbiotic relationship. Lichenscapes don't only look good, they're also barometers of the health of the environment. Ecologists here use London's lichens to monitor air quality and, more recently, the impact of climate change. Plus, insects live in lichen and some smaller birds favour it as a camouflaging, nest-making material. London has over a hundred different lichen species, from the bright orange *Xanthoria parietina* and the apple-green *Flavoparmelia caperata* to the grey, leafy *Parmotrema perlatum*. Globally it's thought there are a whopping 17,000 different lichens.

Mosses, meanwhile, are simple land plants that like damp conditions and will happily blanket rocks, trees and walls. Rather than producing flowers, they reproduce with spores. Generally they are small and diminutive-looking growths, but the unusual bank hair-cap moss can reach epic 30cm heights. The most common moss growing around here, though, is *Dicranoweisia cirrata*, which grows about 2cm high and has skinny leaves. If you find a good, thick patch of it carpeting a sunny wall it makes a great pillow for a resting head.

I do get licks of lichen and mossy patches on my roof, but one of the best places to see both thriving is in churchyards as they love gravestones. A few of us found ourselves in such a place on Halloween. Abney Park Cemetery in Stoke Newington, north east London, is overgrown and full of crumbling statues, with winding paths that lead you through a tiny wilderness which supports much wildlife. Foxes and tawny owls love this place. Late on Halloween afternoon, a group of goths hung around a gravestone, some heavily made-up band members posed for publicity shots, solitary walkers paced and small clusters gossiped on benches. Birds made the cold air sing and our hot breath made it steamy.

This place, which sits, like most green spaces in London, in a heavily built-up and busy area, was wildwood in Neolithic times, and then, when the Romans were in Britain, it was populated by wolves and bears. It later became pasture and woody parkland before becoming a cemetery in the nineteenth century. This All Hallows' Eve, as October gave way to November, Abney oozed a wild kind of magic. The tiny worlds of lichens and moss, crusting and carpeting tumbling monuments to the long dead, seemed all the more intriguing in the spooky twilight. I reverted to my younger self and populated the growths with imaginary mini people, all dressed as witches and ghouls of course.

THE BIKE RIDE

Leaving the house as a nervous city cyclist takes a while. First there's some serious psyching up to be done. This usually involves the studying of online journey planners and the careful plotting of routes that are easy to memorize, followed by the consolation of the pocket-sized and highly portable A to Z street map. It involves dressing for the occasion. Tight trousers and sensible shoes, suede gloves and a patterned head scarf. It involves packing and packing again. Bike lock, keys, lights in case it gets dark, the emergency map. All dressed up and with somewhere to go, I sit and run through the carefully plotted route once more, repeating road names under my breath, an ode to London's confusion of streets, a carefully crafted formula that will get me from here to there.

Finally I'm outside and unlocking the bicycle. This takes an age as I become entangled in security cables and drop the weighty lock on my foot, cursing shoes that aren't sensible enough to take this level of abuse. Finally, I wheel the bike down our side alley, scraping bag and pedals along both walls. My final flourish involves toppling into the neighbour's flowerbed as I make my way down the garden path and out onto the street. Sophisticated, as ever.

Deep breath, then, and I'm off, slightly muddy and officially clumsy, but enthusiastic nonetheless. Wind rushes over my balancing body, my legs stretch and spin, my back curls and nestles into a comfortable riding position. I brace myself against the flow of air, the cars, the buses, the noise. I speed down a busy road before cutting quickly off down a side street and into calm. Feelings of freedom sweep in, of covering uncharted territory. I breeze through some of London's coolly elegant quarters that sit so close to my humble home, with their imposing squares and private, gated gardens.

Zipping through Islington on a gentle, downward trajectory, I soon meet the canal and replace road with towpath. I head east, slower now, negotiating with other bicycles, walkers and runners. Ducks are amusing themselves on water that's laced with floating autumn leaves. I stop and wind my fingers through persistent plants that are breaking through the walls and tumbling over the concrete. Creeping leaves, turning burnt, seasonal shades, blend with graffiti, wallpapering the waterway with colour. The mirrored slick of water doubles the strength of the light, making it stronger, brighter.

A man sits on a bench, paperback in hand, catching some faint rays. Grey blocks loom behind him, towering homes with panoramic views of canal and city. Black coots call from the water, sliding through the grey gloss. Discarded blue plastic bags blow into balding trees and bushes, becoming pinned in the branches and waving like flags. There's a rustle, an echo, a hum. And my discordantly squeaky brakes, warning slow-going strollers of my two-wheeled presence. I wait patiently before passing under a bridge, using the pause in progress to think how pleased I am to have become a city cycler.

WILD EXPANSES AND LOW TIDES

I haven't spent as much time on the roof as I'd like to recently. The weather's been unkind, plus daylight hours at home are getting rarer. But yesterday the sky turned the most brilliant of blues and I stole a few precious minutes in my secret garden. The sycamore tree that looms over it is almost bare now, but still casts the odd leaf adrift. Those final leaves were dancing about the roof in slow motion on Saturday. I kept catching them out of the corner of my eye and mistaking them for brown butterflies.

Despite wild weather, the bulbs and seeds I planted in early October are all doing well. I've got lots of green shoots – leaves of lettuce, spring onions, garlic and flowers. My flat-leaved parsley plants are doing especially well. The tomatoes have just about finished now, the plants are looking withered and wrinkly. There are a few lone fruits left on the vines but I don't expect they'll turn red. The squirrels continue to gnaw at them when they get desperate.

It was almost odd being out there yesterday, momentarily just sitting and looking. After a summer devoted to lounging around, the roof is now starting to feel like less of an escape. Even choosing to have the door open, so fresh air can blow into my bedroom, is a decision to freeze these days. As it gets colder, my roof becomes a much less enticing space. It's still loved; we just don't spend that much time together these days.

At this time of year, one needs bigger expanses of outside space to march across in order to keep warm and to get desirably rosy cheeks. I went for a long walk earlier this week with one of my best friends. It was a weekday treat away from the office, we ate soup in a tiny cafe then roamed over Hampstead Heath in the autumn damp for hours.

A sudden downpour left the leaf fall slick and gleaming, and the lichen on the tree trunks fluorescing lime green. Glossy droplets balled on fat, pink berries. When the rain returned, tree canopies made protective umbrellas over our heads. We searched for and found the hollow tree we'd last visited over two years before. The tree is spacious and bulbous at the bottom; there's enough room inside for two people to sit. It's seriously special. More so that day because it had taken us years to re-find it.

It's incredible how your troubles spill out, how you hear yourself admitting your fears when you walk on the Heath. It's in this place that one has the room to confess and also the shelter. In a rare London spot where nature actually seems vast and mighty, capable of greater things than any human, worries seem more manageable somehow. It's easier to be honest and to listen deeply.

It's the weekend following that invigorating weekday walk and I've headed out west, excitingly on the back of a Vespa. It took us quite a while to get to the Thames at Twickenham, but it's a beautiful day and the novelty of travelling through London on the back of a scooter has kept me thoroughly entertained. We were pulled to the river at this westerly point because we were determined to see the effects of the annual November draw-off, something I had no idea happened until last week.

Each year the weirs at Richmond Lock are lifted to allow the Port of London Authority to carry out essential maintenance works on the lock, weirs and sluices. The weir being lifted allows the river between Richmond Lock and Teddington Lock to drain naturally at low tide and this creates a short, annual opportunity to access the lower shore. The draw-off leaves behind the lowest of low tides, with the river around Eel Pie Island emptying to almost nothing.

We park the scooter and head into the emptied river, slurping around in oozing mud, crunching over hundreds of mussels

and sifting through all kinds of debris. We watch herons standing like ancient statues, wondering where all the water has gone no doubt, and then stalking, disgruntled, across the swampy terrain. Coots and gulls bob in the tiny puddles that remain. A rusting buoy lists naked in the exposed landscape, covered in a green weed that transforms its shape into a globe. The air is damp, hinting at rain, but the light is bright. We walk until we reach water and I discover that my dazzling red Wellingtons aren't watertight.

12. December into Early January

THOUGHTS ON ENDINGS

I've felt more rooted and grown up since moving to this flat and inheriting the roof. I guess it's having things to care for and watch develop, something to worry about other than my own silly dilemmas and neuroses. Since having the roof, I've noticed new subtleties about London too – her many green and brown hues, how the sun tracks across her sky, her light and shade and how much rain falls onto her streets.

So, it's winter once more and my year of aerial edible gardening is drawing to a close. As I write, I find myself at home, hugging a hot water bottle and wearing several jumpers, ski socks and a pair of thick woolly arm warmers. I'm slowly thawing out after another increasingly icy bike ride. It's December now, only 2.30pm, but it's already a little dusky outside and snow is expected later on.

It's the shortest day of the year, the winter solstice, and I'm reminiscing, recalling some of the successes and some of the tragedies of the past year. Top of the success list have to be my red fruits – the strawberries and tomatoes. Sitting here on my chilly perch, wrapped in woollens, I think fondly about the many delicious fruits that hung about my balcony over the summer. Juicy strawberries and tomatoes that were best eaten straight from the vine and warm from the sun.

Second on the success list is the sticky-leaved tobacco plant. Mine were covered in white, trumpet-shaped flowers throughout summer and early autumn. Part of the nightshade family, the night-flowering tobacco plant is closely related to its cigarette-producing cousin, *Nicotiana tabacum*. But, instead of being dried, rolled and lit to create curling blue clouds of smoke, this variety gives off invisible but equally potent clouds of perfume. Often closed up during the day, the flowers open as dusk drops. Excellent marketeers, my irresistible tobacco trumpets fizzed with insect life. I would poke my nose inside them for a powerful blast of fragrance or lie back and catch subtle wafts as they blew about on the evening breeze.

Third on the gardening success list are my runners, beans that wove a wall around the roof and provided me with delicious vegetables throughout the summer. Fourth are herbs and greens, all kinds of shoots that transformed my salads. And fifth is lavender – a fragrant, silver-leaved plant that has made my local bees giddy with nectar this year. Dried sprigs sit in an espresso cup on the bookshelf above me.

The tragedies? The courgette plant I inherited was one – it produced several flowers but only one rather pathetic courgette before suffering a slimy end thanks to some snails. I'm a bit embarrassed by my courgette failure as everyone I know who's ever grown them has declared them to be easy and ended up with more than they could eat. Another tragedy was the cucumbers that never were. I tried to grow them twice but both times I planted cucumber seeds I got a crop of mushrooms instead. And likewise the 'Flamingo Beet' chard that wasn't. I managed to grow only one diminutive plant despite sowing many seeds.

Way back in early spring my bedroom was rather chaotic, as it's the only sheltered place I can use as a plant nursery in my tiny flat. I had a few disasters as my room isn't very big. Early springtime evenings were fraught with danger as I regularly tripped over seed trays, sending soil and sprouts spraying across the carpet.

I've discovered that I like gardening in my pyjamas and that growing something from seed, watching it develop and then eating its fruits is a joy. I've daydreamed on the roof and entertained out there. It's the force behind new friendships that I've forged. The garden has opened my eyes to a whole new side of London and urban living. It has been such an interesting project and I can't wait to hatch a set of plans for next year.

But back to the here and now and, like last month, the time I've spent in the garden in recent weeks has been pitifully minimal. There isn't actually anything to do out there work-wise at the moment. All is fairly tidy, the spring bulbs are in, the winter leaves planted and, yes, it is far too freezing for lounging around. When it's sunny and crisp it's glorious out there, but generally December has been a little gloomy.

This weekend has been different – the roof is a tiny bit snowy and crackling with ice. My brave winter lettuces are dusted with frozen flakes. Right now more snow is starting to fall and I fear slightly for those lettuces and leaves, which were doing so well until this big freeze hit. But it is beautiful here at the moment. My plants have snow beards and the bushes are weighed down with thick icing. It's festive and fine, if rather cold.

A NEW YEAR AND A POSTSCRIPT

I've been in a funny situation with my roof recently. The flimsy wood and glass door that opens out onto it has been stuck shut. For a good few weeks, I haven't actually been able to get out there at all. The only way of accessing my garden has been by leaning precariously out of the bathroom window. From this steamy vantage point I've watched a grey squirrel digging through my pots and occasionally sunbathing in rare rays. I've also spied both male and female blackbird visitors. I know it's not an unusual or exotic species, but I think the ordinary blackbird is my favourite. The male that visits is dishevelled but tuneful, and the lady is plump with cosy, soft brown feathers.

I have the gardening jitters at the moment. I haven't done anything useful on the roof for weeks and I'm now worried my fingers are becoming the most faded kind of green. This week ended with a gin-soaked evening in a dampish basement bar decorated with peeling floral wallpaper. I drank a cocktail called the gardener's tea break from a bone china cup. The damp air, the peeling paper, the name of my potent drink – it all seemed terribly fitting. Toying with my chintzy cup and saucer, I realized I'd been on a break for too long, indulging in London gin rather than London gardening. I need to get soily again.

A long, hard night meant that yesterday was physically something of a write off. But a day spent mainly in bed, glumly watching the sun make my yellow curtains burn with a weird cold heat, did give me a chance to ponder, to think about what on earth to do next with the outdoor appendage.

One wasted day tends to lead to a more productive one and today I was out on the roof early. I finally managed to open the roof door. Sheer brute force and many deep breaths did it. It was bathed in low sun and I was well wrapped up in a thick coat. I did some tidying, moved things around, re-familiarized myself with the roof's spaces and corners as my hands slowly turned blue. I swept leaves and gathered up old bits of string. I stacked empty pots and bunched canes into neat groups. After a grumpy couple of months staring mournfully at each other through condensation-covered windows, suddenly my garden and I are friends again.

This year I'm a girl on a serious budget. I've left my office job behind, to write more and earn less, and so my roof project has now become both more of a necessity and more of a challenge. A necessity because I really could do with saving money by growing my own, and a challenge because, although I've done all my gardening fairly cheaply so far, this year it's simply got to be even cheaper. In this spirit, I've started eyeing up other people's empties.

Some neighbours have been clearing out old furniture and I've acquired a ladder/shelving unit thing that I'm excited about. I have no idea what it was but, with a bit of creative woodwork, I can see it becoming a brilliant planter for salad and herbs. My very own ladder of leaves. I also managed to acquire three large paint pots that had been dumped by a bin. They'll make great, deep containers once I hammer in some drainage holes.

I've also decided that this is the year I grow baby carrots in that pair of leaky red Wellingtons and the year I grow potatoes in a hessian sack. It's the year I install a section of guttering to grow lettuce in and the year I have much more success with courgettes and radishes. It's the year I consider compost more and wonder whether a wormery would work. It's the year I work my hardest to convince at least one person I know to raise chickens. It's the year the roof becomes twice the jungle it was last year.

SELECTIONS

A Few Things I Grew and How They Fared

BASIL – cheat. I tried to grow basil from seed but wasn't successful. As a disappointed basil lover, I cheated and ended up nurturing a large, supermarket-bought plant.

BAY – easy. It was important to include some trees on the roof, be they tiny ones. The bay tree was low maintenance and extremely hardy. I hope we are together for a long time. A bay leaf is a good addition to any winter casserole, making it much more flavoursome.

CORIANDER – also easy. This cut and come again herb tasted gorgeous raw in salads, as well as lightly cooked. The flowers were white sparkles and left behind strong-tasting seeds that could be dried, crushed and used to flavour curries and stews.

EVENING PRIMROSE – stunning seedheads. These plants were a colourful addition to my night planting. Shop-bought plugs sent up tall stalks and flowered throughout summer and early autumn, and even survived the winter. The pretty seedheads, dried, decorated both my room and roof.

FLAT-LEAVED PARSLEY – fast growing. At first we didn't get on, the taste not quite to my liking. I persevered and we became firm friends. Its strong, almost bitter leaves became a staple in all my salads and as a garnish. It was a hardy crop, which kept me in fresh leaves during autumn and winter as well as summer and spring.

FRENCH BREAKFAST RADISHES – all flower, no fruit. They grew well, but I only harvested one radish due to being overly sentimental. The plants bolted and bloomed, so pulling them up became a violent, de-flowering act. The bulbous seedpods looked brilliant, both on the plant and then dried and arranged dramatically in an old bottle. Next year I must be less sensitive.

LAVENDER – a hero. Silvery, grey and even almost blue, this bushy, spiky-looking plant was incredibly easy to look after, barely needing any attention. Drought resistant, it flowered in late summer. The purple prongs danced with bees and smelt divine when brushed against. I saved and dried the flowers and used them to decorate my room in winter.

LUPIN – disastrous. It was incredibly dapper at first, with star-shaped leaves that twinkled with dew, but ultimately this plant was a failure. Slugged to within an inch of its life within days of moving to the roof, it never recovered, withered and died. Not sure I will try again.

MINT – magic. I grew two varieties of mint on the roof and now want to try out many more. Thirsty but keen to multiply, my plants seemed to get bigger and bushier the more leaves I plucked from them. Mint is my new favourite drinking partner.

ROCKET – peppery perfection. Rocket made every salad superior, tasting particularly good with tomatoes and strong cheese. Not as easy to grow as I thought it would be, possibly due to my impatience and not leaving the plants alone long enough to establish. I actually had most success growing this crop over winter. A hardy species, I grew my biggest and best-tasting plants when the weather was cooler.

RUNNER BEANS – a great success. The runners formed a heaving wall on one side of the roof. In spring they were strung with tiny, bulb-shaped flowers that looked like ruby fairy lights and were beloved by bees. In summer, they were strung with long vegetables that looked just how runner beans should and were beloved by my friends and me. Delicious steamed and eaten a little crunchy.

SALAD LEAVES – for the impatient, space-poor gardener. Throw a few seeds in any kind of container, sprinkle with soil, keep dampish and within weeks you'll have endless supplies of home-grown salad. The strong-tasting and good-looking mixed leaves that I grew beat anything I'd previously bought wrapped in plastic and sealed in a vacuum.

STRAWBERRIES – a minor triumph. These loved their hanging basket abode, producing big glossy fruits. The berries lasted about five minutes once ripe, and the plants then spent the summer sending out lots of runners. Next year I must grow more.

TOBACCO PLANTS – my absolute favourite. Not edible but enchanting. The big white flowers glowed in the dark and smelt sweet. The tall, dried stem and seedpods of the dead plant looked pretty on the roof throughout winter, especially when iced with snow.

TOMATOES – a joy. These were a labour of love and a source
of immense pride – there's nothing like bringing them up from
seed, sharing a bedroom with the seedlings and then seeing
them graduate to outside space and watching them become
strong, handsome plants. They cropped at the end of summer
and into early autumn, and every day I ate one was a good day,
especially as the weather got cooler and winter felt like a threat.

Most Beautiful Moments

Dawn breaking and the sun pouring gold over the East Reservoir.

A smashed window glinting on the Market Estate, Holloway, looking like a spider's web made of glass with buildings caught in it.

Owlets nestling up against the rain in an ancient oak tree in Kensington Gardens.

Damp Highbury Fields at the end of winter, the grass dotted with bright crocuses and the trees full of noisy flocks of birds that swell and swarm.

Insomnia sound-tracked with early birdsong.

Torrential rain, sun, then two rainbows caught between tower blocks on the Woodberry Down estate, Hackney.

Long, quiet, midsummer afternoons solo on the roof, with just the sun for company, surrounded by growth.

Walking home along Tufnell Park Road, the hot air thick
with the smell of jasmine and rose, a heady summer perfume
mingled with a touch of exhaust.

Dusk. Red wine. Chelsea Physic Garden. A plague of toads
and frogs.

A moth-wing breeze that beat across my left cheek, early on
Sunday morning before bed.

Pyjama-clad gardening. With wild hair. And fuzzy vision.

A quiet moment on a sunny brick wall, resting a sleepy head
on a pillow of moss.

The door to the roof open on a stormy night, snail trails on the
bedroom carpet, silver slime against dark blue weave. Slightly
horrifying but strangely pleasing.

Clumps of grass growing out of the side of buildings.

A dusty-looking moth dancing in sodium yellow light outside
the Kwik Fit garage on Camden Road.

A circle of plane trees with tremendous, thick trunks and wide spreading canopies, growing straight out of the tarmac in Lincoln's Inn Fields. A large, dark, bracket fungus sitting like a bookshelf on one trunk.

Lupin leaves covered in dew balls.

Lichens printing monochrome pavements with patterns.

Things to Read

Ackroyd, Peter, *London: The Biography*.
    London: Chatto & Windus, 2000.
Carson, Rachel, *Silent Spring*.
    Boston: Houghton Mifflin, 1962.
Deakin, Roger, *Wildwood: A Journey Through Trees*.
    London: Hamish Hamilton, 2007.
Macfarlane, Robert, *The Wild Places*.
    London: Granta, 2007.
Sackville-West, Vita, *Let Us Now Praise Famous Gardens*.
    London: Penguin, 2009.
Selby, Amy (ed.), *Growing Stuff: An Alternative Guide to
    Gardening*. London: Black Dog, 2009.
Shepherd, Allan, *Curious Incidents in the Garden at
    Night-time: The Fantastic Story of the Disappearing
    Night*. Machynlleth: Centre for Alternative Technology
    Publications, 2005.
Various, *Granta 102: The New Nature Writing*.
    Summer 2008.

Places to Go

Abney Park Cemetery, South Lodge, Stoke Newington High
Street, London, N16 0LH
Website: www.abney-park.org.uk
Nearest transport link: Stoke Newington railway station

Arcola Theatre, 27 Arcola Street, London, E8 2DJ
Website: www.arcolatheatre.com
Nearest transport link: Dalston Kingsland Overground station

Camley Street Natural Park, 12 Camley Street, London,
N1C 4PW
Nearest transport link: King's Cross St Pancras Tube station

Chelsea Physic Garden, 66 Royal Hospital Road, London,
SW3 4HS
Website: www.chelseaphysicgarden.co.uk
Nearest transport link: Sloane Square Tube station

Columbia Road Market, Columbia Road,
London, E2 7RG
Website: www.columbiaroad.info
Nearest transport link: Hoxton Overground station

East Reservoir Community Garden, 1 Newnton Close,
London, N4 2RH
Nearest transport link: Manor House Tube station

Gillespie Park, Gillespie Park Local Nature Reserve,
191 Drayton Park, London, N5 1PH
Nearest transport link: Arsenal Tube station

Hackney City Farm, 1a Goldsmiths Row, London,
E2 8QA
Website: www.hackneycityfarm.co.uk
Nearest transport link: Hoxton Overground station

Hampstead Heath, Nearest transport link: Hampstead Heath
Overground station/Highgate Tube station

New River Walk, Islington. Begins at Canonbury Grove and
ends at St Paul's Road

Regent's Canal, especially between Angel and Broadway

Market. Begins at Little Venice and ends at the Limehouse Basin

River Lea, especially between Chingford and Hackney Marshes. Begins in Leagrave, Bedfordshire and ends in Stratford, London
Website: www. river-lea.co.uk

Roots and Shoots, Walnut Tree Walk, London, SE11 6DN
Website: www.rootsandshoots.org.uk
Nearest transport link: Lambeth North Tube station

Spitalfields City Farm, Buxton Street, London, E1 5AR
Website: www.spitalfieldscityfarm.org
Nearest transport link: Whitechapel Tube station

Walthamstow Reservoirs, Ranger's Office, Walthamstow Reservoirs, Thames Water, 2 Forest Road, London, N17 9NH
Nearest transport link: Tottenham Hale Tube station

Woodland Walk, from Finsbury Park to Highgate. Begins at Alexandra Palace railway station and finishes at Hampstead Tube station

Thank You to

Timber Press for asking me to write this book.
Kitchen Garden magazine, for first giving me the opportunity to
write about my garden.
The Wildlife Trusts, and particularly London Wildlife Trust,
for inspiration and knowledge.
My friends and family, for being endlessly
enthused by my growing and writing ambitions.
And Ria, for being a fantastic flatmate.

Index